911 TO HEAVEN

MIRACULOUS MOMENTS THAT REMIND US WE ARE NEVER ALONE

PATRICIA CRAMER

Copyright © 2026 Patricia Cramer

All rights reserved. Except for brief quotations used in reviews or articles, no part of this publication may be reproduced or transmitted in any form or by any means without written permission from the author or publisher.

ISBN (Paperback): 978-1-886881-01-3

Published by: MacBridge Publishing

This is a nonfiction work. Any stories shared are used with permission and reflect the experiences of the individuals involved.

CONTENTS

Foreword   vii

1. God's Wonderful Coincidences   1
2. The Kindness of Strangers   41
3. God Helps Those Who Help Others   67
4. The Children are Always Protected   89
5. God's Little Whispers: The Inner Voice   107
6. Visions of Angels   147
7. The Awe of the Unexplainable   159
8. Love that Lives Beyond Death   197
9. The Messages in Dreams   219
10. God's Special Gift: Grandparents   239

Afterword   255
Index   257
About the Author   267

For Ed
Who was persistent about my calling.

For Nancy and Kathy
Who were in the right place at the right time.

FOREWORD

God's serendipity...a tremendously comforting thought for a tired and weary world. Everywhere around us each day is violence, anger, wars, murder, dysfunctional families, abandoned and abused children, road rage, despairing and homeless people, addictions of every kind, and stressed-out humans. The greatest balm for these wounds would be love, compassion, kindness, respect, altruism, and joy.

The gift of God's little daily miracles brings us these very things. When we look for a blessing, an unexpected kindness from someone else, even the sense that an angel has been sent to take our hand, that touch of God's love brings with it such happiness. A sense of peace can take hold in the midst of chaos. As we become more joyful, we begin to spread more joy around us in every encounter. Our world desperately needs these blessings in abundance.

The people you will meet in this book are all just ordinary people...exactly like you and me. I met them in my travels as I was presenting seminars nationally and internationally; I met them at social gatherings and business meetings, at places where friends got together, and sometimes randomly in a line somewhere. The amazing stories of these people brought me to both laughter and tears. Mostly, these examples of God's wonderful workings in our daily lives bring comfort and peace.

What is required to look for the small miracles is a greater openness on our part–more awareness and less tunnel vision. We need a willingness to expect with great anticipation and gratitude: "Dear Lord, give us this day our daily synchronicity...and not just daily bread..."

After all, it has been promised to us. Psalm **91**, verse **11** is explicit: *"God has set His angels over you and charged them to guard you in all your ways. In their hands they will bear you up,'lest you dash your foot against a stone."* So, we CAN expect miracles, we CAN anticipate help, we CAN call upon that wonderful promise and we absolutely CAN send out our **911** to heaven!

1

GOD'S WONDERFUL COINCIDENCES

"Wow, what a coincidence!" How many hundreds of times have you heard someone utter those words? You probably have spoken them yourself. Usually, the speaker is expressing delight at some fortunate turn of events, something perceived as "lucky" or positive for that individual. Many people think of coincidences as random, "fortuitous," or unexpected occurrences. We seem to be excited when they happen, but don't particularly have a sense of expectation that they SHOULD happen.

On the contrary, coincidences are a manifestation of a partnership in timing between the earthly and the divine. If we think of "co" as "with," and "incidence" as a "happening," the word itself creates an idea of "happening with" or partnership. God allows circumstances in our lives where the partnership of human and divine melds, and we see direct intervention into earthly circumstances. Rather than being **unexpected**, it is a blessing that is ***frequently and lovingly given***, and we should both <u>expect</u> and <u>anticipate</u> these blessings. What is required from us is a greater awareness on a regular basis of the wonderful things that God is doing in partnership with us all the time. Many of us walk through life obliviously, not actually seeing the small miracles all around us.

People who effectively "tune in" to this idea experience "fortunate" things frequently; they are simply more attentive to the blessings being given. On the contrary, those who create a mindset of "I'm really unlucky, nothing good ever happens to me" will find pessimism in most of life's circumstances because they will be blind to the divine partnership. They will miss the moment where God's action in their lives is most immediate and personal.

One of the ways that we learn to increase our awareness of the "co-incidences" is to develop an attitude of appreciation for even the small things that happen every day. As we become more alert to seemingly mundane events, we find that there are wonderful, "lucky" things happening daily; but they are <u>not random</u>, and they shouldn't be a surprise. Then, occasionally, major blessings are given, those miraculous experiences that transform our lives and sometimes even <u>save</u> our lives.

God periodically uses other people to affect us in unusual ways and when they follow his promptings, they are a blessing for us and the source of the "co-incidence." They or we may not even understand the leading being received, but when we obey, we are a source of comfort and help to those whom God is acting upon. A young woman told me once of the day that she stood at the bottom of an escalator in a downtown department store idly looking at clothes on a rack, consciously thinking "What on earth am I doing here? I'm not even interested in any of this stuff." However, she continued to stand there a moment longer. Suddenly shrill screams came from overhead and as she looked frantically around, she saw an elderly woman who had fallen near the top of the escalator and was trapped with the moving stairs injuring her. The escalator was right next to the rack where she was standing, and no one else was nearby. She bounded up the escalator, and helped the lady escape. Store personnel arrived shortly after that, but her presence had allowed the woman to escape sooner than if she had waited for the employees, thus lessening the extent of any injuries.

A coincidence that she was there to help? Absolutely. IF you see it as a coincidence of God positioning her to be in the right place at the right time. Could it have been a random event? Anyone who believes that God plays an important role in everyday life would say it is <u>not</u> random. It is the melding in one moment in time of human and divine.

In many of the real-life stories you will read in this chapter, you will see the repeated thread of God placing people *in the right place at the right time.* Since God sends His angels as messengers and helpers, they sometimes seem to be nudging us to get to the "right place." It is the promise of Psalm 91 verse 11, "God has set His angels over you and charged them to guard you in all your ways. In their hands they will bear you up, lest you dash your foot against a stone."

Whether God sends one of His angels to help in a moment of need, or inspires a human being to be His instrument, the driving force is love. When people are led to act in a way that helps others, they may be a human instrument, but it is Divine inspiration. We usually associate the heart with the emotion of love, so these actions are truly coming from the hearts of angels, both earth "angels" and heavenly angels. How blessed we are to receive this gift.

∼

Sherry L., Arizona, Entrepreneur

Will Sherry's desperately-sought flowers appear in time?

"It was Christmas. I awoke to pouring rain and dreary gray skies that wept unrelentingly. What a contrast to the cheerful mood and brightness in homes everywhere that contained happy families, laughing children, gifts, decorations, music, and food. My soon-to-be husband and I were alone this day, having sent the children off the previous day to their father in California as we did every other year. Our own family celebration had been on the 22nd, a happy occasion with a big dinner, gifts, my parents, and assorted friends. On this dreary, wet Christmas day, around 11 a.m., I called my mother and stepfather to wish them an "official Merry Christmas" even though we had celebrated it just two days before. I was distressed to find my mother in a severe emotional crisis over some ongoing family problems. "We'll be there in 45 minutes," I stated firmly. No, she insisted, she didn't want to spoil my day too, and she felt she wasn't in any shape to see people. No way was I going to accept that! I'm really close to my mother and she had raised me, her only child, as a single parent. When you love someone dearly and that person is in distress, there just isn't any other choice, you must be there! And Christmas is supposed to be a happy day after all.

Ken and I started out resolutely through the downpour, despite being "dis-invited" and not having told her, "It doesn't matter, we're on our way..."

I desperately wanted to bring mom flowers...something cheery on this miserable, stress-filled day, to show her how much I loved her. It seemed hopeless; every store was closed, streets were flooded and empty, and the rain was unrelenting. No flowers anywhere... As Ken was saying that he was sorry but flowers seemed to be out of the question, a calm "knowing" came over me. I just knew that I would, indeed, find what mother and I both needed.

Then I saw her! A flower lady, standing at the upcoming intersection, with a bucket filled with bright, beautiful flowers in her hand. Just standing in the grayness like a beacon...I couldn't believe it! I jumped out and bought everything she had.

Thanking her profusely, I asked, "Why on earth are you out in this terrible weather?" I'll remember her answer forever... "I'm here because there are mothers who need flowers on Christmas..."

What a memorable day after all. What I'll always carry in my heart are two strong, visual memories: first, the look on Mom's face when she saw us on her doorstep with a huge bouquet, and second, the sight of that flower lady in the mist, our Christmas angel."

Laura Z., Arizona, City Administration

Laura's life is saved in two amazing incidents in high school, both examples of divine timing.

"One day I went to school early, arriving at 6:30 a.m. to prepare for an important chemistry class. As I crossed the street, a car came from nowhere and I barely had time to look, horrified, realizing I couldn't get out of its way. Suddenly, I was shoved roughly away from the car as it swerved to avoid me. When I got up I was shocked to see a boy named Chris standing there, someone who was in my class but never showed up at school before 8:30.

Chris told me that he had awakened at 5:30 a.m. with an overpowering urge to go straight to school. Since he didn't usually get up before 7:30, he laid in bed trying to avoid the feeling, but found he just couldn't ignore it. He was nearing the crossing about the same time I was and saw the car coming straight toward me. Chris remembers thinking, "I'm too far away; I can't reach her!" The next thing he knew, his hand was making contact with my body as he pushed me to safety. This was certainly not something that could be accomplished except for divine intervention."

Laura's life was saved a second time under the most unusual circumstances.

"One other example of remarkable protection occurred when I was driving with friends. Five of us were in the car, a driver and three people in the back seat; I was riding in the front passenger seat. As we approached the intersection close to school, I jumped out suddenly and said, "I'll just walk the last block." The driver kept going and no one from the back seat had time to move up to the front.

The driver took the next right turn less than 45 seconds after I got out of the car. A cement truck pulled out of a blind driveway in the park and smashed into the front passenger side of our vehicle. The impact was so severe that the crushed passenger door was touching the gear shift. When the police arrived to investigate, an officer asked why the front seat was empty. My friends told him, "She just got out a block farther back..." The officer said, "That must have been a miracle because otherwise she would be dead." I was in shock about how close a call that was since I had never before jumped out of the car to walk, and in fact, never did it again."

Laura feels that she had an example of divine intervention in her childhood also.

"My mother had a strange and disturbing dream in which I drowned wearing a smocked dress. I had a dress like that, so my fearful mother threw it away. It was found later in a closet because another family member had pulled it from the wastebasket and washed it, thinking it had fallen in there accidentally. My mother was shocked to see it in the closet again and, determined to destroy it, cut it up with a scissors. Imagine her distress when another smocked dress was given to me as a birthday present. Undaunted, she cut up the second dress.

Sometime after that, my mother took me with her to visit some friends on a farm. While the children played, my mom left briefly to see other friends not far away. She had been gone only a short time when she felt an overpowering need to return to the farm. Stopping to call the friends she was on her way to visit, mother informed them that plans had changed and she wasn't coming. In a state approaching panic, she hurried back. Imagine her horror when she saw me clad in a blue and green plaid smocked dress (not mine) preparing to go with the others for a swim in a nearby pond. I had gotten my own outfit dirty, and my mother's kind friends had dressed me in one of their daughter's outfits. My mother said, "That's it. We're going home" and bundled me out of there. It wasn't until much later that she told me of the circumstances that had given her such terrible foreboding. We both believed it was possible that my life had been spared that day."

Kamila L., Michigan, Massage Therapist

A young couple's family is guided to their home from out-of-state on the night of a devastating miscarriage.

"I fell down an entire flight of stairs when I was four months pregnant and had a miscarriage. This was a very traumatic thing made even worse by the fact that I couldn't contact my husband and had a friend take me to the hospital. Nobody knew this had happened to me except the friend. Later that evening I told my husband who looked at me in shock and said, "I knew something had happened to you today." We just sat there together crying and trying to put the pieces of our life back together knowing that our dream of a family wasn't going to happen right then.

Suddenly, we heard a knock at the door and discovered his entire family--mother, grandmother, sister, aunt--standing there hesitantly saying, "We don't know why we're here exactly, but just had the strongest feeling that you needed us tonight." Now this wouldn't be so unusual if they had just lived across town, but you have to understand that *they had traveled for three and a half hours from out-of-state on a weeknight with no advance notice*! This was simply unheard of! My husband's family NEVER visited except on a weekend, and then only when there were considerable planning, advance telephoning and pre-arranged schedules. Strangely enough, they had left their house on a weeknight without calling us, not even knowing if we were home, something that had never occurred in all the years of our marriage.

Yet, that night their support was so terribly important to us, a comforting presence surely inspired because God knew that a consoling hug was badly needed. Time has healed some of the pain, but the vivid memory of the night that divine guidance led our loved ones to comfort us has stayed with us over these intervening years." Kamila continued with a story in a slightly different vein. "One other unusual situation that occurred in our family happened at the time of my grandfather's death. He was terminally ill with cancer and in the hospital at the same time that our minister's son was admitted with a dangerously high fever that was putting the little boy's life in jeopardy.

All of us kids went to visit grandpa and took him a bright balloon that we had decorated with band-aids to cheer him. After we left, grandpa insisted on being wheeled to see his young friend; for he and the minister's son had always had a very special relationship. Although the little boy was barely conscious, grandpa spoke to him, tied the bright balloon around his wrist, and said "As long as this balloon is tied here on your hand, you'll be just fine. Please believe me about this."

Even in his serious condition the youngster seemed to understand and be cheered by grandpa's presence. With that, my grandfather left to return to his room in a very weak state, and in fact died that night. At about the same time grandpa died, his young friend's fever broke and doctors said that the boy would recover with no problem. The balloon was still tied to his wrist, a silent testimonial to the love of one old man for one young child.

Oh, and by the way, we found out about this exchange between grandpa and the minister's son when the minister told the story as part of grandpa's eulogy at the funeral. I assure you, there was not a dry eye anywhere in our family as we all wept together."

Linda C., Arizona, Professional Consultant and Speaker

A series of fortunate events saves the lives of several young people.

WhenLinda's middle daughter, Julie, was just 21 years old, she was involved in a life-threatening accident that ultimately had a happy ending because of a series of extremely unusual "coincidences."

Julie and her friends were returning from a trip to California when they pulled off the main road for a rest stop and went the wrong way on a desert road as they started out again. Their traveling companions in the second car had not stopped at the same time, so they were now alone. This stop had occurred in the area around Palm Springs where the large wind-driven windmills are constructed.

The group was unfamiliar with the dark road, and suddenly the driver went off the shoulder of the road, overcorrected getting back on, crossed over and hit a berm. This caused the Toyota Tercel to flip end-over-end to the front, fly over a six-foot fence just grazing the top, and come to rest 70 feet out in the desert among the wind-turbines. All three passengers were ejected through the front passenger-side window.

Linda continues with the story: "The force of being expelled through that window tore Julie's clothes off and tossed her through the air about 30 feet where she landed against a fence that stopped her, thank goodness. At this point the car was on its roof with one solitary headlight beaming steadfastly into the now eerily-quiet darkness. It was probably around 10 p.m. at this point and the three victims were unconscious.

Within minutes, a car came down the road. Its occupant was going to work on a midnight shift, and tonight he was (for the first time in his life) about 45 minutes early. He saw the single beam way out in the desert off the road, and rather than ignoring it as some kind of reflection, he stopped his car, and walked close enough to realize that this was an accident scene. Some of the young people had begun to regain consciousness and were moaning. He couldn't see anything, and knew he wouldn't be able to deal with this without some light and/or equipment. The good Samaritan raced back to his car, and drove at breakneck speed to his jobsite at the power company, about another five minutes away.

By extreme good fortune, his coworker who was an ex-EMT (emergency medical technician or "paramedic") was also at work early, and the two men took a truck equipped with special lights back to the accident scene. They were able to use the lights to locate all three of the victims, and the paramedic training immediately warned the rescuers to cover Julie who would otherwise have been a victim of hypothermia.

The men called the hospital in Palm Springs which (coincidentally?) had a well-regarded special trauma center and prepared to treat them. I was told later by the doctors that two of the three accident victims (one of which was my daughter Julie) would have died if they had not been found when they had been. The fact that they were found almost immediately allowed the doctors to take care of injuries that would otherwise have been fatal. Julie was in terrible shape. She had internal as well as brain injuries, and almost everything was broken, including pelvis, thighs, femur etc.

Julie spent a considerable amount of time in critical condition in the intensive care unit. As I sat there many days waiting for her to become more lucid, it became apparent that because of the brain damage, her mental state was like that of an eight-year-old.

There didn't appear to be any understanding of "time" except for one peculiar detail. She became fixated on the expression 9:00. Everything in her world revolved around 9:00. For example, she would say, "I have to eat at 9:00," "I'm going to have surgery at 9:00" (She wasn't), or "I have to go to sleep at 9:00". Although annoying, we couldn't become frustrated with her because we were just glad she was talking, even if it was nonsense statements.

Her boyfriend Clay, who was one of the other occupants of the car, was in a coma for four days, and she kept repeating endlessly the statement, "Clay and I have a special bond." The odd coincidence that happened was that Clay came out of his coma at 9:00 in the evening, and Julie never repeated either of her phrases about 9:00 or the "special bond" ever again. She seemed to lose her two fixations at that moment.

The aftermath of this accident was quite severe. Julie didn't walk for four months, and had to relearn a lot of basic skills that everyone else just takes for granted. She lost much of her independence because she needed others to accomplish simple tasks and had to move back home where there were people around her. Through it all, however, she has maintained an extremely positive attitude, has never indulged in self-pity or whining, and is grateful for every day she's alive. We are too."

Diane J., New Jersey, Board of Education

After many futile attempts, a loving and dedicated sister is given time with her brother just hours before he dies.

Diane's memory of her brother's death is a bittersweet saga of how close-knit siblings were reunited just before they were physically separated forever. Diane and Louis were as close as twins, often feeling the same things, sharing thoughts that needed no words. A juvenile diabetic, Louis made it to the age of 33 before his health began deteriorating rapidly. His wife suddenly became furiously possessive, reluctant to allow family members to visit or to talk to her husband. Diane remembers one heartbreaking time when she went all the way to the house, and her sister-in-law refused to let her go inside.

Diane left the house thinking that she would never see her brother again, and began to sob hysterically as she sat in her car in front of the house. "What happened next had to be some kind of intervention from God where he sent angels to help me. I suddenly felt the most unimaginable kind of peace, so penetrating that it filled every inch of my being. I felt more than heard the words, "Everything will be alright." As soon as I had this experience, my attitude changed abruptly, from one where I had worried and fretted, to one where I let all uncertainty go, and exuded a quiet strength and calm.

While on the surface nothing changed, inside I had changed...I simply never worried again. On January 13, my sister-in-law needed someone to look after Louis while she was at work, so she took him to my mother's. This was very unusual. For the first time in a long time, we had uninterrupted time with this special person, a brother and a son. My mother spent the day with him and called me over in the evening. We talked, laughed, read, dozed, and cried a little and none of us realized these were Louis's last few hours on earth.

When his wife came to take him home, as my mom and I walked Louis to the car, he suddenly slumped in our arms as we went down the front steps, and he was gone at that moment. We were so grateful that after many months of being denied any time with him, the angels arranged for us to be able to spend those last few precious hours together. We know that his wife had no idea that he was so weak and near death. The angel that promised that "everything would be alright" came through for us in a dramatic way which we will always remember."

A similar story of a reunion that happens with a most unusual timing appears next in Barbra's story, the tale of a daughter who did not have a relationship with her mother for 30 years, but became her mother's caregiver before a death from cancer.

Barbra W., Louisiana, Home Health Care

A daughter's love transcends all else...

Barbra was adopted at three days old by a distant relative and was told at the age of eight that someone else was her birth mother. From then on, she did know her birth mother's name, and was aware that she had nine older brothers and sisters some of whom she saw periodically, but she wasn't really a part of their family. Barbra did not at that point have any kind of relationship with her birth mother, and on the few occasions that they encountered one another, her mother even acted somewhat hostile toward her.

When Barbra was over 30 years old, she began to develop a warmer, more personal connection with her birth mother and started to rebuild the mother/daughter bond. This developed over several years into a close and caring relationship. When Barbra saw her mother's name as a client in the files of the home health care agency that employed her, she was surprised to learn that her mother was ill. In fact, the day that her mother became desperately sick, it was Barbra who went to her house and got her to the doctor. From the doctor, she learned that her mother was seriously ill with lung cancer caused by the asbestos in her apartment. From the specialist they consulted next, she learned that the cancer had spread and her mother was expected to live six months.

At that point, Barbra and her husband insisted that her mother come to live with them so that she could have full-time care. Though her mother had raised nine children, it was the daughter who didn't know her for thirty years who assumed the burden. Barbra says, "One day we were sitting in the kitchen and the conversation turned to the topic of forgiveness. Mom said, 'That's why I'm here, you know.' I felt as though she was asking to be forgiven for not raising me although she couldn't bring herself to say exactly those words. Somehow, I just knew the question that was in her heart and I didn't have any reluctance at all to say to her 'I forgive you, Mom.' She seemed happy with that. And although we never really talked about why she gave me up, and to this day I do not understand the circumstances that led to the adoption decision, it truly doesn't matter anymore. She did what she had to do and she had her reasons; I cannot be bitter about what happened since it was beyond my control.

Things became more difficult toward the end because Mom went through stages before dying: denial, anger, withdrawal, and combativeness at times. Often, I just tried to calm her by repeating 'I love you, Mom; I love you, Mom.'

I had the strangest experience one night approximately a week after she died. I awoke in the middle of the night, and saw a vision of my mom just standing across from my bed. I blinked, startled, but it was still there. As I looked at the vision, I felt a strong sense of peace and comfort washing over me like a tide, and I knew that I was being told that Mom was fine and not in any more pain. I knew too that she loved me very much despite the mistakes and problems of many years.

I am convinced that God brought my mother back into my life for a reason, and I thank Him every day for that wonderful blessing. I am a better person for having gone through all of this, as painful as some of the things were when they happened, and I am grateful to God for all of it."

Dale C., Arizona, Transportation Industry

A man avoids the horrible accident that kills his friends.

"At one point in my life, an incredible coincidence kept me from being killed in a freak accident. After our usual Friday football game, several of the team members and some of our friends were discussing our plans for the weekend. One of the guys, Tom, invited everyone to his house the next afternoon to shoot baskets, and about a half dozen people committed to going.

At the last minute, I had something come up that delayed me, and this also happened to two other friends who had to cancel. Tom's parents asked him to go and pick up his sister and her girlfriend at a riding stable, so the guys who were there stopped shooting baskets to run the errand. On the way back, a drunk driver slammed head-on into their car and killed all five of the kids inside. The three of us who had been unable to come at the last minute escaped the crash that killed our friends.

The family that lost both its son and daughter at the same time found this to be a bizarre postscript to a story of trying to create a safer environment for their children. They had moved from a large urban metropolis on the opposite side of the state to a small, quiet, conservative town less than two years earlier after losing their two oldest children in a head-on crash also from a drunk driver. For one family to lose all four of its children to automobile accidents within a span of two years is heart-wrenching beyond belief.

The parents dealt with their grief in a most unusual way. A dentist and a homemaker, they started taking in children from the local high school, especially ones who were troubled and came from a background of abuse or neglect. They acted as guardians and foster parents, and permanently adopted at least one of the kids who lived there. In addition, the members of our senior class adopted them as a second family, and not a day went by that someone wasn't there with them.

I also want to relate one other incident in my life that has always been very significant to me, although not necessarily a coincidence. When I was eight years old, I fell out of a tree and smashed my left arm beyond recognition. The physicians at the emergency room strongly recommended amputation for two reasons: 1) they didn't feel they could restore it and 2) they felt that it would be very difficult to heal and likely useless for the remainder of my life.

My mother refused to allow this and fought the doctors forcefully, insisting that they try to set the arm and get it to heal. This was in a period of our history where people typically didn't question doctors. And yet she was the one who was right! The disfigured arm eventually healed despite massive scarring and I had probably 60% use of it for many years."

Marilyn G., Minnesota, Airline Industry

Marilyn would have been on a plane that crashed except for a power failure.

On December 1, 1993, a Northwest Airlines commuter plane flying from Minneapolis to Hibbing, Minnesota crashed near its destination, and tragically, all 18 passengers aboard were killed. Marilyn tells of a colleague, also a Northwest employee, who traveled four nights a week on that flight, commuting between a home in Hibbing and her workplace.

The colleague's department had a serious power outage the day of the disaster, causing her to cancel her regularly scheduled trip home that night and thereby saving her life. "Since she had to stay and get her department back in order, she didn't use her reservation. Except for that one strange coincidence of the power loss on that particular afternoon, she too would have died."

Dr. Bobbe Sommer, California, Author: Psychocybernetics 2000, Psychologist, Speaker

Several fortuitous circumstances lead to publication of a new book.

A series of unusual "coincidences" led Dr. Sommer to the opportunity to update the excellent work of Maxwell Maltz. Dr. Sommer attended a lecture by Maxwell Maltz that transformed her life. It was somewhat of an accident that she even went to the program because it was an extra ticket given to her by a friend, Teri Cole Whitaker. She had not specifically planned to attend that lecture.

Dr. Maltz was speaking about following your passion, living your dreams, doing what makes your heart sing, creating an energized life... He asked several audience members very pointedly "Are you doing what makes your heart sing? Bobbe became introspective at that point and thought, "No, I'm not." She pondered for a moment what she had done with her life...go to school, get married, have a family, set up a practice; all things that she felt others expected her to do. She had a successful therapy practice, but wanted to reach a broader audience with speaking and consulting.

At that very moment, she decided to live a more passionate life by becoming a speaker and trainer. That one moment changed everything!

She set out on a journey of building her speaking business and became so popular that Working Women magazine chose her as one of the 10 hottest speakers in corporate America. As a result of that article, she received a call from network TV asking her to do a six-minute interview with Maria Shriver. Ms. Shriver asked her during the interview if she had any turning points in her life and Bobbe spoke of the influence of Maxwell Maltz, and how she had altered her career based on hearing him speak. She told about how she had gone on to study his principles and incorporate them into her training and speaking.

Shortly after that broadcast, because of the national exposure, Bobbe received a call from Nova University in Florida which was conducting a nationwide search for an author to update Maltz's 1960s work. Nova University had created the Psychocybernetics Foundation because they had been given the rights to his research, papers, and manuscripts upon his death. The search committee asked if she would be in Florida anytime soon to interview. Just 10 days away, she was scheduled to present a seminar near the University with a free day for travel blocked into the itinerary. She used that day to interview with the committee and was ultimately chosen to author Psychocybernetics 2000.

Did Bobbe experience just a series of lucky coincidences, or did she live out a truly guided experience? She feels that it was not just random, fortunate circumstances but a larger plan that she followed for growth, because she believes in guiding forces in our lives. Many people will benefit now and in the future from the contribution she has made in the area of psychological thinking and study.

Examples of UNUSUAL TIMING

The following stories offer intriguing examples where the people involved did not understand why or how they acted as they did. It was the results that proved that even if they didn't comprehend why circumstances occurred as they did, God's plan was still in operation.

Marilyn M., California, Administration

A woman packs up almost every possession she owns just hours before a devastating earthquake.

Just before a devastating earthquake hit the Northridge area of Los Angeles on January 17, 1994, Marilyn experienced a most incredible series of events that changed her life. After renting the home she has lived in for the last four years, she had just closed on the purchase of that same house Dec. 29, 1993.

For years, the owner had refused to sell the house, but Marilyn felt strongly guided in October of 1993 to again make an offer despite the chance of being rejected one more time. She had seriously prayed about this decision and even talked to people at her church asking for advice. A certain dollar figure kept coming into her mind as well as being mentioned by others as the offer she should make to the owner. It seemed outrageously low...$80,000 less than the last appraisal, but still she had the conviction that it was the right thing to do.

"The day that I called, our landlord said that she had just learned that she was being transferred out of state, and would indeed be interested in now selling the house. Not only that, but she immediately accepted our offer without countering! We felt that this was unheard of. We were considering taking out a federal government loan for veterans, but were not happy with the terms which included many fees and even points. I told my husband that he should check into the state-sponsored "Calvet" program rather than applying for a federal loan.

We qualified for the "Calvet" loan and found it to be superior in every way for us, and closed at the end of December. We had decided to do some repairs and remodeling, and had begun in January; in fact, we had painters coming in Monday, January 17. The day before, on Sunday, I felt an irresistible urge to protect everything and took down pictures and mirrors, packed away all the crystal and knick-knacks, and taped shut the doors and drawers in my cabinets before covering them securely. I wrapped the most delicate pieces in quilts and blankets and placed them beneath beds. All of the furniture was stacked in the middle of the rooms around lamps, vases, and other small items and then covered with tarps and plastic. Less than 12 hours later, a major earthquake did tremendous damage in our area, and many of our friends and neighbors lost all of their most treasured possessions, while I lost only some everyday china and glassware that was still in the kitchen cupboard. All of my treasured heirlooms and collectibles were safe and sound. One of my friends came over later and said that I could not have prepared any better for that earthquake if I had been specifically forewarned! I honestly cannot explain the driving urge I had to keep covering things and packing others away; it doesn't seem like a typical thing to do when you have a little painting done.

The best part of all is that our "Calvet" loan, obtained just two weeks earlier, included a homeowners' policy with earthquake insurance. It had a $250 deductible, something unheard of for most Californians, so we were able to repair any damage we sustained.

I feel that I was totally guided and protected through the whole terrible experience that devastated other people, but not us. I don't think it was just luck, because if our home had still belonged to the previous landlord, it would have been demolished, we would have lost all of our breakable possessions, and we would have had to move out right after the earthquake."

Roberta B., Arizona, University Administration

How did the loaded gas tank stay on as long as it did?

"At one point in my life, I was a member of a Christian musical and drama troupe that did quite a bit of traveling, and we had a really strange experience as we returned from a road trip. We had loaded two full tanks of gas at the beginning of the trip home and had only traveled about a hundred miles, so we still had a lot of gas left. We were traveling in a large motor home, and as we got back to the headquarters and pulled into the garage, after everyone had left the vehicle, one of the gas tanks fell off the bottom with a terrible crash. We all were very scared as we realized that if the tank had fallen off the motor home or been dragged along the road in transit and created sparks there would have been an explosion. We were all certain that we had been protected from danger."

Ginger V., Arizona, Computer Operations Specialist

A discussion of "blessings" is interrupted by a near-accident.

"Something happened to me once that seemed like the strangest of coincidences, but thinking about it over time has raised the possibility that maybe more than coincidence must have been involved.

I bought a new car and my son and I were driving together, when the talk turned to the topic of "blessings in your life." My son was playing the role of a skeptic, saying that people didn't deserve or receive blessings, when the point was driven home in a most unusual way.

At that moment, the car ahead was going very slowly, maybe 20 mph or less in a 40 mph zone. I wasn't upset but decided to pull around and pass it. After I did so, I saw in the rearview mirror that the slow car fishtailed, swerved dramatically, crossed over all the other lanes, and went off the road into a field.

At the moment that all of this was taking place, there were no other cars in its path, and I realized with a jolt that if there had been any other cars nearby, including mine, there could have been an accident. My new car, of which I was so proud, could have been wrecked.

To me, the point was reinforced, that you can be blessed and helped, and I relayed that to my son. He may not have been totally convinced, but the look on his face told me that he had at least started thinking a little about different possibilities."

Marilyn S., Oregon, Financial Industry

Was it just a coincidence that Marilyn's husband answers the phone?

"My husband works the graveyard shift and gets home around 5:30 in the morning, and immediately falls asleep instead of staying up. One morning, I had a flat tire on the way to work and called home to get him to help me. I couldn't get him to answer so he must have already been sound asleep. I called my boss to let him know that I would be late, and then tried his parents' house for help. No luck there either.

When I finally called him the third time, he did pick up the phone. I said with surprise, "I can't believe you're awake. I tried to reach you before and you didn't answer." He told me, "The only reason I'm awake is because I felt somebody physically shaking me just before the phone rang. But there wasn't anybody here." I think the angels must have awakened him because they knew how desperately I needed his help."

Paula T., Arizona, Customer Service

A missed hair appointment narrowly avoids a potential encounter with a gunman.

"I had a friend who overslept one time and missed a hair appointment and was really furious at her kids for not waking her up. It was hard to get those appointments after all. When she drove over later to schedule another time, she was quite surprised to see a yellow police-line barrier up around the shop. Imagine how she must have felt to find that a disgruntled spouse/boyfriend had come with a gun and shot up the beauty salon and killed or injured several people at the exact time that she would have been there getting her hair done. She could easily have been a victim that morning. She did feel that she had been protected from harm."

Wendy S., Minnesota, Credit Union employee

Students are kept from a potentially dangerous situation.

"My sister was on a high school band trip in New York City and was part of a large group composed of probably 150-200 students. They were taking a harbor cruise that showcased some of the special New York sights such as the Statue of Liberty, and then on to Ellis Island among other noteworthy places.

One ferry could not take the entire group at once because of the number of other passengers already boarded, so the student group remained behind to wait for the next boat on which they could all be together. The original boat that might have had the students aboard, except for that one simple decision to wait, carried a severely disturbed person who attacked quite a few passengers with a knife causing serious injuries. They all felt extremely lucky that they were not on that ferry, because some of the students might have been hurt."

Jennifer F., Oregon, County Services

Did Jennifer foresee the flat tire?

"I was driving with my husband one time, and out of a clear blue sky said to him, "What would I ever do if I had a flat tire while I was driving along like this?" It just seemed to pop into my head as a matter of curiosity. He was nice enough not to say that weird things seemed to pop into my head, and he simply answered the question, telling me how one would handle that type of situation.

I couldn't believe it when, just a few minutes later, we actually did have a blow-out while I was speeding along. I just did exactly as he had described to me and we came safely to a stop.

We both thought that it was quite an odd coincidence that I should have been asking about that right before it happened."

"Bill T.", Michigan, Regional Manager-Automotive Company

Bill ends up in the right place to meet his current girlfriend.

"There was a time in my life where things were not going very well. I had been struggling with some unexpected medical problems, and then was suddenly informed by my wife of 16 years that the "thrill was gone" and she wanted a divorce. I ended up burying myself in my work to escape some of the pain, and so I was doing quite a bit of travel.

I came home one Friday night and was invited out for some drinks and a few laughs with one of my best buddies who told me to meet him at one of the "trendy" hotel lounges. The jerk never showed up, so I decided to leave.

On my way home, instead of turning off at the freeway exit I normally use, I abruptly drove in the opposite direction and stopped at a dance club where I had absolutely NOT intended to go. Even as I did it, I found myself wondering why I was doing this, but felt strangely drawn to the club.

I looked around to see who was there and saw an intriguing-looking woman at a very large table, but did not speak to her because she appeared to be with someone. Because I had been very interested in speaking to her, I was surprised when she came up and asked me to dance. I discovered that the interest was mutual and she was not attached at all but had come to the club with a singles group after a sports event. She had simply been sitting there with another member of the group. Great! "Penny" turned out to be a very interesting and unique person, and we spent the entire evening dancing and talking and promised to get together again. This chance meeting has blossomed into a wonderful, supportive relationship that has been tremendously helpful in getting over some of my life's recent "bumps."

I believe that all things happen for a specific purpose, and am continually amazed at the number of coincidences (or maybe not...) that brought us together: my plane could have been delayed and I would not have gone to meet my friend, I could have said I was too tired when my friend originally invited me, maybe he would have shown up, I might have gone straight home without stopping at the dance club, I might not have seen her in that crowded room, or her group might have gone to a different dance place after their game. So many chances for our relationship to have never happened... Therefore, I believe it was meant to be and will serve a purpose in both our lives and will enrich us in a way that will allow us to make a more significant contribution to humanity.

Erin A., Oregon, Banking

Erin returns home unexpectedly to find a startling thing.

"Four years ago, I was married and working part-time as an Office Manager. One day, I went to work after dropping off my daughter, and out of the blue, I got this terribly strong feeling that I should go home because something was awfully wrong there. I tried to ignore the feeling because this was not very convenient...it was a 30-minute drive back and forth, but it kept increasing in intensity.

Now, there shouldn't have been anything to worry about. My husband was at home packing for a camping trip with his friends, so everything should have been fine. I kept wondering, "Why do I have to go home?" Finally, I couldn't ignore the feelings any longer, and so I took that long drive home because I had the feeling that I should NOT call!

Guess what? My husband wasn't packing for camping...he was packing period! He was leaving me and taking our household goods, cleaning out personal papers and bank books etc. I arrived in time to stop some of the damage, but if I had remained at work, I would have lost everything. I think the angels were looking out for me and my daughter."

Jene B., Arizona, Environmental Health

A woman receives comfort from a radio station.

"One of the most interesting things that happened to me that I have no explanation for occurred on an emergency trip for my husband. I had taken him to the V.A. Hospital about 190 miles away for a closed esophagus. When we got to the V.A., the situation was so serious that they wanted to transfer him by ambulance to a larger hospital at the state capital and wanted me to follow in our car. I was tired and stressed and recovering from a recent angiogram myself. I been up all night, driven for four hours already, waited anxiously at the first hospital, and now faced driving another two hours. It was pitch black and a horrendous thunderstorm was raging outside. And I am not fond of driving at the best of times, so both my husband and I were worried about my being able to do this.

As we started out, I did a most uncharacteristic thing. I reached over and punched a button on the radio and instantly heard a woman's voice saying, "This is K-A-L-M, calm radio." She spoke soothingly for a few minutes and then thanked us for joining her and told listeners to be calm. Now this wouldn't have seemed so odd except that my husband and I rarely, if ever, played a radio in our car, and this vehicle (although used) was new to us and we had never programmed in any stations. Even if we had pre-set favorite stations for our own town, this was a strange city so they would have been different. It had to be pure chance that the station I picked up was that one. Or was it? It was certainly the perfect message for me to hear at that moment and it made me feel so much better. I did, indeed, calm down and drove safely with the ambulance ahead of me.

Ever since then, when I think about this situation, I believe that maybe God or his angels were trying to help me. It worked!"

I would like to add a curious postscript to Jene's story. I met her when she attended one of my training seminars, and a most unusual thing occurred. One of the exercises I use for this program has participants paired off into teams discussing a topic of their choice. The teams are decided randomly by having half of the people pick a name tent of one of the other participants from a "deck" that is fanned out like a deck of cards. Jene randomly picked the name tent of a young woman on the other side of the room. She chose her husband's ongoing battle with the "blocked esophagus" as her topic and was surprised by the other woman's reaction.

Her partner, a woman half her age, has a husband in his thirties with the identical problem, and they are currently facing the same surgery that Jene and her husband had just gone through. Jene was tremendously helpful to this young woman, calming her worries, and warning her about some of the things they might face. Of all the people in the room who might benefit from what Jene was discussing, it had to be her young partner, who was extremely grateful for the information. This simple incident reminded me yet again that God and our angels know exactly what we need at any given moment, and if we but ask, it will be given to us.

Nancy V., Minnesota, Furniture Sales

Three friends communicate simultaneously.

"I have a couple of very close friends who live really spread out across the country, in Virginia, Michigan (where I lived then), and Texas. One time, I had a very strong feeling that I needed to write or call my friends, and when I went to my mailbox there were envelopes from both friends waiting for me. Stranger still, I had received the identical Hallmark card from each of them.

It seemed like too much of a coincidence to ignore, so we all connected by phone, and were there to console one another since one of the women had just lost her father. It was a happy coincidence and reminded me of how truly important our friends really are."

Adrienne S., Arizona, Retired

A daughter's sensitivity tells her that her father is in danger.

"I had the most extraordinary coincidence happen in my life. I had gone out with friends to a club, and the group of girls I was with that night all went out to eat afterwards. We had ordered our food, but it hadn't arrived yet when I suddenly was gripped by an intense urge to go home immediately.

I told my friends that I needed to leave and they tried to discourage me, telling me that our food would arrive soon. However, I wouldn't be dissuaded, so they finally left with me and went to my house.

My mother was standing on the porch as I drove up, and she said to me "Go into your father right away; he's having a heart attack." Sure enough, he was in very bad shape and in fact, died three weeks later. I have always been amazed by the intensity of the internal message that took me to my father's bedside at the very moment he needed me."

Evelyn N. (Evie), California, Retired housewife

Evie knows when her friend dies despite none of the staff being willing to tell her.

"I was in the hospital for a hip operation and spent several days with a roommate who had the same first name as mine. Evelyn C. was in the hospital for a minor operation on a small tumor in her colon. We just really enjoyed each other's company and had so much in common that the time passed quickly and we even made plans to see each other when we were both out of the hospital.

The day of Evelyn C.'s colon surgery, she went off to the operating room with no qualms at all. She was very relaxed and confident, having been told by her doctor that this was no big deal and she had absolutely nothing to worry about. I was moved to a different room during the other woman's surgery but when Evelyn C. came back from recovery, she was placed in a room directly across the hall from me.

I noticed that the other Evelyn's family spent the evening with her and left after 11 p.m., at which time she was fine. I dozed off but was abruptly awakened around 11:30 and I remember the time because I checked my clock.

As I lay awake, I saw a magnificent, iridescent pink veil float into my room, then brush across my face, continue floating to the other side of the room and then through the outside wall. I was wide awake at that point, blinking into the dimness, thinking I had just imagined something here. I felt a lonely sense that I didn't immediately understand, and then a kind of dread when I heard CODE 6 being called on the intercom.

I saw staff hurrying into Evelyn's room across the hall and I called out to them asking if she was alright. Eventually someone came in and said for me not to be concerned but to go back to sleep. I had this bad feeling, however, and found it almost impossible to sleep because I just didn't believe that things were OK.

I found out the next morning that Evelyn C. had died at 11:30 the night before and I think that maybe she was trying to say goodbye to me. One thing is kind of strange...pink was Evelyn C.'s very favorite color, and that is what I saw floating. I believe that some other-worldly hand woke me up at just that moment so that I could say goodbye. I've not really told this to anyone else because it seemed so strange."

Karen S., Michigan, Window Company

A mother senses her son's death.

Karen had a 63-year-old brother who died from lung cancer. No one had told her mother, who was an invalid in a nursing home and very frail, that her brother was even ill because they didn't believe she would understand or be able to cope with it. She was not lucid for much of this time. They had not yet informed her of the death, and were trying to break it to her gently on the day of the funeral. The remaining children sat one on each side of the bed, and held her hands, ready to impart their sad news. Before they spoke a word, she began to ask questions: "Why isn't Richard here?", "My chest hurts", "Richard's sick, isn't he?", "Richard told me he wouldn't be coming back here" (that one really freaked them out), and "What happened to my Richard?"

The family knew that in her own way she had somehow sensed something was wrong even though she hadn't been told anything.

Mimi B., California, Graphic Design/Video Animation

Mimi is saved from a rolling vehicle in a most amazing way.

"My Jeep stalled right near the entrance to a gas station, and I wanted to push it out of the way, so I called for some of the employees of the station to come and help me. For some reason, I thought the people were behind the car positioned to help me push it as I steered. I put the gear in neutral and discovered to my horror that I was the only one holding the vehicle...the others weren't in place yet.

With a lurch, the Jeep began to roll backward as I stood by the open door leaning inward to steer it. I was knocked down and the car rolled right over the front side of my jacket as it lay open and came directly up to my arm that was outstretched. It *barely touched the underside of the arm and then stopped, and did not roll over and crush or break my arm.*

I really don't know what stopped it at that point, if it was just luck, or gravity, or somehow the helpers had gotten their act together. I do know that I was extremely fortunate and believe that maybe there was also a little heavenly help involved.

I think that God takes special care of things because of another incident during the January 1994 earthquake in Northridge. At my parents' house, a beautiful crystal "Madonna and child" statue fell off the mantle onto a marble hearth and did not break despite every other piece of glass or china in the entire house being smashed and broken. How could only one piece be saved?"

Karen J., California, Office Manager

Karen has experienced many strange incidents in her life.

"I have had so many "coincidences" in my life that I no longer believe that they are in any way random, accidental, or arbitrary. Instead, they somehow weave together to make up the fabric of my life.

When I was just 16 years old, I knew before my parents that my uncle had died. I went to spend the night with my cousin, and I heard his voice, although no one else did. I believe this was an indication that I had some sensitivities that others do not have. I have experienced very strange happenings such as having a niece who was given up for adoption at the age of 5 find me again when she was 16.

I was trying to purchase a condo, and had missed the one I wanted because I was late on my offer, and yet I happened to see another one just "driving by" which gave me a wonderful, warm feeling. I just knew that it would be mine, and the purchase of that one went off without a hitch.

My job at a law firm started out as temporary and then became permanent. My boss, who was a woman, started getting very nitpicky, and it made me so unhappy that I decided to start talking to headhunters and leave. But a weird thing happened.

The woman who was driving me crazy had an accident and was off work for quite a while and then decided not to come back. I was given a new position with a new boss, and can now exercise a great deal of creativity and have become a tremendous resource to the company. Here I had almost left my job, and now I am a major contributor to the organization and am very happy.

While things sometimes seem to work out in weird ways, they usually do resolve themselves in our best interests. My goal is to be guided and led in a way that I will be in the right place at the right time doing the right thing."

Reflect and Act

Reflect:

- Think of a time when someone was able to help YOU in a way that seemed like a coincidence.
- Think of a time when you were placed in circumstances where you were able to help, support, or rescue SOMEONE ELSE.
- When you are in a situation to be able to help

someone, what makes you <u>CHOOSE</u> to help rather than just being an observer or walking away?

Act:

- Look for ways to be more "tuned in" to the needs of someone you could help by being a better listener.
- Actively practice being more present on a daily basis to the world around you.
- Take a small step by offering your aid to someone the next time they express a need for help, or when you see a situation where you could step in.
- Take a moment at the end of the day to reflect if you missed opportunities, or if you stepped in when God placed you "in the right place at the right time."

2

THE KINDNESS OF STRANGERS

People have been helped in the most amazing ways. Sometimes it's hard to determine whether the source of the aid is an angel in disguise or a human who has been led to be in that place at that time to help. Both possibilities have occurred. In the stories that follow, you'll see examples of aid where strangers have appeared out of nowhere and disappeared more quickly than is <u>humanly</u> possible. These strangers have rescued stranded hikers, flooded vehicles, frightened children, and women alone and in difficult circumstances.

At the same time, there are real-live humans who have turned up for other people and rescued them from situations for which they did not have the ability or resources to help themselves. These helpers are not required to render aid, but have done so from a generosity of spirit that sets them apart from the typical person on the street. You will read about: an air conditioning technician who spots a drowning child from a roof, someone who befriends scared teens in a foreign country, a man who simply by listening helps a suicidal mother change a decision to end her life, and a nameless gambler who reunites a young woman fleeing from rehab with the family who loves and supports her.

John R., Arizona, Retired Communications Analyst

A repairman on a roof saves a child's life.

"I was buying a set of tires, and when I gave my address to the owner, a surprised look crossed his face: "Why, you live right behind me," he said. I didn't recognize him, but that wasn't at all unusual, since the seven-foot brick walls dividing the properties often prevented you from meeting your neighbors. The very walls that provided privacy to swimming pools and patios set up impenetrable barriers to neighborliness.

Suddenly, the tire shop owner asked me what seemed to be a strange question. "Did you have a compressor installed on your roof a few years ago?" I responded with a puzzled "yes," because a few years before we indeed had replaced the air conditioning compressor. I wouldn't find out until today, however, that the day that repair was done, a miracle had occurred. I remembered for a moment that I had occasionally regretted having placed the unit on the roof in the blazing Arizona sun. Why hadn't I located it on the ground east of the house in the shade of a large tree? I thought later that the air conditioner would be far more efficient in a shaded place than in its exposed position on top of the house.

I was shocked at what was said next. The tire shop proprietor said quietly, "If it hadn't been for that man working up there on your roof, my son wouldn't be alive today!" I listened intently as tears filled his eyes and he told me an incredible story. His baby son Danny had just learned to crawl, although he didn't typically move more than a few feet at a time. Without his knowledge, Danny had crawled through the open sliding door and tumbled into the family swimming pool.

The technician working on my roof had apparently heard the splash and peering down from his unique vantage point, had seen the baby in the pool. Racing down his ladder and through the yard, he discovered a locked gate on the neighbor's side. Undaunted, he scaled the seven-foot concrete block wall, dove into the water, and rescued the limp child. The father choked as he said that he wasn't even aware of the situation until the technician knocked on his door holding the soaked baby. Unable to do more than cry uncontrollably, and numb with guilt, it was some time before he could regain his composure and thank the air conditioning man.

Surprised and puzzled, I blurted "But he never said a single word about that to my wife or to me! I had no idea that such a thing had happened." Inside I was thinking, "Talk about an unsung hero..."

From the day the tire store owner related his amazing tale, I have never had a single moment's regret about the roof-mounted air conditioner. Clearly, God had a very special reason why it had to be that way. If my unit had been installed on the ground, there would have been no one to see or help the endangered infant.

Kathy D., Arizona, Teacher

An unusual stranger helps lost hikers.

Kathy, her husband, and her son went on a camping trip outside of Tucson with another family. They had a great time and on the last day, Kathy's son David elected to extend the trip by hiking down the mountain with the father and son in the other family. The others planned to return by car. Kathy and her husband had no reason to worry since the other family had considerable hiking experience, although the back side of Mt. Lemmon is acknowledged to be quite strenuous and a challenging hike. David and his friend were both 10 years old at the time. The group had a map, had planned a route, and expected to be home by 6 p.m., for what was supposed to be a 12-hour day because they started at 6 a.m.

As David reported later, the group encountered some difficulty when the trail was much rougher than expected, and poorly marked, not matching the map for Catalina State Park. The tiny group forged onward with no cell phone and not much food, although they did have water. By the time they should have been home, they were still on the mountain as it began to get dark. he three stopped by a stream and climbed onto some large rocks which the afternoon sun had warmed.

On Monday morning, the hikers set off bravely again, although by now they were out of food and somewhat discouraged. By this time, Kathy had called out the Search and Rescue team, fearing that someone had fallen or some other horrible catastrophe had occurred. The search included a posse and a helicopter which focused on the Sabino Canyon side of the mountain, which is the one more commonly used for hiking. People coming down the trail were questioned about seeing the group, but answers were negative time and time again. Some people did call with leads, but each time they ultimately amounted to nothing. Kathy became more frightened with each passing hour.

Meanwhile, David, his friend, and the father started on their way again Monday morning but by now were going in the opposite direction of where the search efforts were being concentrated. They were tired, hungry, and very lost; they had absolutely no idea where they were. At one point, a helicopter passing overhead stirred action–the group screamed, jumped up and down and waved their arms. By the direction being traveled and the obvious lack of interest in ground activity, David and his friends decided it was simply a commercial helicopter headed north on a routine trip to Phoenix. It didn't appear to be a helicopter looking for them.

The three were now on a back road out of the mountains heading in the general direction of the town of Catalina, following a wash. About noon on Monday, a pickup truck appeared on the road rather suddenly and offered to take them into the Circle K in Catalina. Ecstatic, the group accepted the ride because they had not seen any other sign of humans or civilization and this appeared to be their best, and only, opportunity for rescue.

While the Circle K employees got them drinks, the stranger offered some change for a phone call and then disappeared before they could thank him. The father and two boys described the stranger and asked who he was so that they could contact him to express their appreciation. Despite a thorough description of the man and his vehicle, no one knew who he might be and none of the employees had seen him come into the store with the lost hikers. Catalina is an extremely small town, the kind where everyone knows every other person, and nobody seemed to know the helpful stranger.

After David was reunited with his family, the local television station wanted to do an interview segment. Because several serious and even fatal hiking accidents happen every year, the station thought it could be an excellent educational piece to warn other potential hikers about dangers. During the interview, the families requested the station to ask the rescuer to come forward so they could thank him, but no one ever responded.

David's strongest memory is of consciously praying for help, praying for a solution and a rescue. He believes that his prayer was heard in the person of the kind stranger whom no one had ever seen before.

Amy K., Paraguay, Student

Mysterious strangers help the stranded car.

"My family and I and another man (a missionary) had just left church, venturing into flooded roads from the heavy rain that had occurred. We thought we could make it okay, but soon encountered one particularly awful road where we didn't have any other choice except to continue cautiously forward. We held our breath as the water level crept higher and higher, soon reaching the car doors. In one scary moment things got worse when a bus drove right past us too close and made a huge wave sweep over the car. Now we were really frightened! But a strange thing happened to me just then; in the middle of feeling really scared, I <u>absolutely</u> knew that God would take care of us and we would be alright.

Immediately after the wave washed over us, the car stalled from the flooded engine, so then we were stuck unmoving in the middle of the road. My dad took charge and asked the other man to steer while he jumped out to push the car–with a broken wrist! It was a recent injury that had just happened the week before, so it couldn't have been very well-healed yet. Poor dad started pushing with one arm and we didn't move at all!

I looked around to see if anyone could help him but didn't see a soul–everyone was surely in their houses trying to stay dry. I closed my eyes tightly and began to pray very hard, "PLEASE God, send someone along to help us get out." As I looked out the back window, I saw two men coming toward the car; it seemed they came out of nowhere. They called out to my dad that they would help him push the car, and with those extra hands, we immediately began moving forward out of the flooded area. When we got out of the high water, my dad wanted to offer them some money for their help, but when he turned around no one was there. I mean they were gone! We all looked at each other in disbelief, wondering how they could go away so fast and were left with one inescapable but incredible idea–could these have been angels? We were all just so amazed at the thought. We took a moment to give a heartfelt prayer of thanks and then drove safely home. I thought this was so awesome!"

Joyce W., Minnesota, Accountant

Joyce and her friends discover a serendipitous helper in a deserted parking lot.

"Several years ago, I went with a friend and the friend's daughter to a seminar (where, interestingly enough, the topic of angels was one of the discussion points...) and we stopped at a Target store afterward. We were the last to leave the store, and walked out into a deserted parking lot, discovering to our dismay that we couldn't get our car to start.

As we looked around, we became a little worried because the store was locked, there was no telephone available, and nothing nearby was open. We stood there talking about what we should do when we saw someone walking directly toward the car, which was near the center of the completely empty lot. A man approached us, quite dirty and unshaven, and extremely poorly dressed, and he offered to help us. We were all a little nervous, but at this point we didn't have other options, so we said we would appreciate anything he could do. The stranger asked if he could sit in the driver's seat, and I specifically remember my friend discreetly grabbing her purse and moving quickly out of the seat and away from the car.

Whatever the man fiddled with inside the car did the trick and it roared to life. I was standing on the driver's side as the man got out of the car, and I looked at him saying, "Well, you're just our angel." He smiled a funny, secret kind of smile and walked away, and as we watched, he simply faded away in front of our eyes.

One minute he was there and the next minute the lot was empty. There wasn't anything to hide behind, and the huge empty lot was too great a distance for him to walk across to escape our view. All three of us were rather startled to think that maybe something otherworldly had just happened to us."

Theresa B., Arizona, Administrative Assistant

A frantic prayer is answered.

Theresa related an unusual story of a routine stop at a convenience store that turned into a few moments of terror and then relief.

"I was working late one night and had to stop for gas at 12:30 a.m. on my way home. I had filled my tank at the Circle K and gone inside to pay the clerk. At this point, nothing out of the ordinary had occurred except that a police car that had been at the store pulled away as I drove in.

While I was paying at the counter, I heard the door open and I was aware that someone had entered the store and was walking through the aisles. I did not turn around, but felt a crushing sense of dread and a presence of evil. It swept over me from nowhere. I was convinced in one extreme moment of clarity that I could die. I remember looking up at the clerk, who seemed unconcerned, and thinking, "What are we going to do?"

I stopped for a moment, and prayed silently and frantically, "Dear God, I have young children, please, <u>please</u> don't let me die right now!" That certainty about death was so strong, I cannot even fully describe how <u>suffocating</u> it felt. The blood pounded in my temples, my throat closed up, my pulse raced, and my knees felt weak as my stomach flip-flopped. I had still never turned around to confront the source of my fear.

Suddenly, I heard the door open again, and a rush of relief swept over me. I turned my head, glancing over my shoulder, and was aware of a uniform–a police officer had come into the store. My conscious thought was, "But that is strange to have another officer come by immediately when one has just left." The sense of relief was unbelievable...I felt protected from harm and knew I would be alright.

I finished paying for the gas and left knowing that something very unusual had just happened. I did not see a police car outside the store, as I climbed back into my car. I became convinced that an angel had entered that store in the guise of a police officer to be there when I needed help.

I tried to explain the intensity of my feelings to my husband when I got home, but I couldn't seem to make him understand. He sleepily said, "So you were getting gas and a cop came into the store. Happens all the time." How could I describe the gratitude I had been feeling all the way home? I simply did not have words to explain that. I slept fitfully that night, awaking several times drenched in sweat, knowing that I had been given a second chance at life. The gratitude continued, and over time, the conviction that I met an angel that night has only grown stronger."

Christina O., Arizona, Administrative Clerk

A mysterious helper appears to help an injured pedestrian.

"While I was living in New York City, I was walking on Park Avenue in the rain and I slipped on a manhole cover. Since I hit my head when I fell, I was dazed and disoriented, but I did notice that people were walking past without stopping to try to help. I had rolled toward the cars and wondered vaguely why no one cared if I was struck and killed.

Suddenly a somewhat darker-skinned man with a distinct accent and a brown trench coat appeared next to me, bent over solicitously and helped me up. He walked me to the sidewalk and asked if he could help me get to the bus. I told him no, but was so badly shaken that I just started to walk away. I realized that I might have seemed abrupt but was really very grateful that he stopped, so I turned to thank him. My good Samaritan had disappeared into thin air! It was only a second that I had turned away, so he shouldn't have been gone that quickly...I began to believe that he was an angel who touched me for just that moment."

Iris S., Minnesota, Communications Consulting/Language Training

Did Iris jump, or was she pushed out of the path of danger?

"I had a medical condition in which I was going blind--I had already lost sight in one eye and had only partial sight in the other--and had a great deal of difficulty accepting the reality of this. One time, I was waiting at an intersection for the light to change, and stepped off the curb to cross the street. A vehicle that I found out later was a taxi started to back up, and although I couldn't see it, I could hear it coming directly toward me. Suddenly in front of me, a huge Black woman appeared who was wearing a full-length calico-type dress with long sleeves, a turban, and high button shoes. This was very strange garb for midsummer in the South Bronx. The large woman bumped me hard and sent me flying onto the sidewalk and out of danger. Nearby people helped me up and helped to gather up the things I had dropped.

I asked, "Where is the woman who saved me?" Some people said, "There was no one near you. How did you jump back onto the sidewalk so quickly?" Others said, "I saw a woman standing there, but she disappeared." I do not know how to explain that some could see this woman and others could not.

I do know that the woman I saw was someone who had appeared to me before when I was a child. I had seen her in a dream at a time when I had severe foot and leg pain and she said to me, "Little girl, drink a tea with "hierba buena" (also called yerba buena, a type of spearmint plant) and your pain will go away." I asked my mother what this was and she indeed did know of it, because it is a member of the mint family and is fairly commonly used as a digestive tea. The woman who had appeared had spoken in Spanish with a distinctive lilt and unusual dialect. So, we made a tea and my leg pain disappeared as I drank it regularly. Since this woman has been with me since I was young, I know that she must be some kind of special protector and helper.

After the incident I described in the intersection, I had my eyes diagnosed and discovered that the problem was irreversible. My mother began praying fervently that I would improve and slowly I started seeing lights and colors. Approximately three months later, my sight was restored and my eye problem had disappeared."

Karen B., Arizona, Administrative Supervisor

Exchange students face a lonely and terrifying ordeal on a bus in a foreign country.

Karen was an exchange student to Belgium at age 17 and was traveling in England with a fellow student. They had spent a fun evening in London at a theater and were returning to their hotel approximately 10 p.m. Karen preferred for safety reasons to take a taxi back but her friend balked at the expense and so they set out walking.

As they passed a bus station, they abruptly decided to take the bus instead, but weren't sure of the route or where to get off. The two friends asked another rider where to disembark and were assured that they would be told, so they decided to relax and enjoy their view of the lights of the city from the second level of the double-decker bus. As the fellow passenger got up to leave, the girls said, "Remember, we need to know our stop." "So sorry," the other replied, "you've already missed it, but don't worry, the bus goes around the same route a second time, and you can just get off the next time." With that, the passenger left.

Disconcerted, Karen and her friend eyed the neighborhood they were entering and realized with a small stab of worry that the surrounding area had become considerably dilapidated. The bus moved deeper into the deserted territory and the girls' nervousness increased with each passing minute and each passing block.

Suddenly, the bus stopped and the lights went out. Now what? Karen and her friend decided to go downstairs and speak to the driver to let him know of their dilemma and their need to find the hotel. The sympathetic driver told them they could certainly ride to the appropriate stop, but his schedule required them to wait for 30 minutes before starting the next circuit. They would just have to wait.

The two girls started back upstairs but Karen had a strong feeling that they should sit on the lower level instead. They found a seat downstairs and apprehensively watched some of the activity outside their window, specifically a gang of unruly teenagers brandishing what appeared to be some kind of blow-torches.

At the end of a very long 30 minutes, the driver turned on the lights and opened the doors to a raucous crush of teenaged bodies pushing through the back door and up the stairs to the upper level. The wild young people jostled and shoved each other, shouting profane oaths, knocking on windows, and stamping their feet on the floor. The deafening noise forced the driver and ticket-taker to go upstairs and try to stop the chaos, while Karen uttered a silent prayer of thanks that she and her partner had earlier chosen the relatively safer downstairs level. The butterflies had not, however, stopped performing aerial stunts in her stomach.

Karen continued, "At this point I prayed silently that we would quickly and safely get out of this strange and difficult situation. A man unobtrusively boarded and sat down in the back part of the bus, but seemed curiously unconcerned about the crashing and banging going on above. In fact, he had a kind of quiet and serene strength emanating from him, just patiently sitting there looking straight ahead, saying nothing.

The ticket officer unexpectedly ran back downstairs with a distraught look: a gang member had hit the bus driver with a bottle and he was injured. As the transit employee went for help, the youths scrambled noisily down the narrow stairway and milled around outside the bus banging on the window where we were sitting. In fact, I had to duck once fearing the window would break. At that point we both were quite afraid.

Finally, the ticket official and a Bobby returned with bad news...the company was sending the bus driver to the hospital and not dispatching another driver that night so there would be no second route and we would have to get off. We were in shock as we left the "security" of the bus--how would we get home to our hotel?

At this point, without asking us any questions, the quiet man sharing the lower level of the bus with us said he would find us a ride, and he disappeared supposedly to make a phone call. While he was gone, a beat-up old car appeared, and the driver asked "Do you need a mini-cab?" There wasn't any kind of identification validating it was a real cab and we felt uneasy about this person, so we firmly refused and moved away from the vehicle.

Then our benefactor appeared again and we told him about the recent arrival of the car claiming to be a mini-cab. He was relieved that we had refused to get inside, warning us that we were supposed to verify the telephone number that we had called with the driver of any mini-cab we ever entered. We learned that since these mini-cabs were an alternative to regular taxi service and could be any kind of vehicle without identification, they were a favorite way for criminals to drive around randomly picking up trusting young women who were then assaulted.

The kind man who had come to our aid obtained a cab, paid for it, and sent us on our way to the hotel. Was he just a nice citizen, or was he a heavenly assistant who showed up in a moment of desperate need and saved us from imminent danger? We thought we were helped by a very special visitation that could not necessarily be explained as a typical good Samaritan."

Joyce B., Arizona, Administrative Assistant

Joyce finds herself in unusual circumstances, able to offer aid during a terrible accident.

"I was part of a large caravan of seven or eight cars attending a Pop Warner football game in Wickenburg, a town west of Phoenix, Arizona. We were a most enthusiastic and supportive group...my nephew played on the team, my sister was a cheerleader, and the rest of us applauded loudly. I was riding in the last car in the caravan with my brother and sister-in-law, my niece, and one of my niece's friends. We dropped out of the string of vehicles at one point to clean up the mess made when the two girls spilled the water bottles they had been playing with. That stop of only a few minutes made all the difference in the world.

Shortly after we got back on the highway, a horrendous accident occurred right ahead of us. A pickup truck ran off the road, overcorrected, and rolled over from the momentum. We were horrified to see this, especially since the passengers flew out through the windshield. This particular highway was living up to its reputation as one of the most dangerous roads in that area.

Our car immediately pulled over to help. The car that stopped right after us had in it a nurse who knew the woman in the damaged vehicle. While the nurse tended to the critically injured mother, I comforted the 12-year-old twin girls who were less badly hurt but extremely frightened and worried about their parents.

I couldn't help but think that if we hadn't stopped for a moment to handle some unintended water spills, we would not have been able to aid the accident victims. Also, there may have been a possibility that our car could have been affected by the vehicle rolling over since we were at the tail end of the car caravan. I think that God arranged for us to be there in that place at that time to assist."

Deborah F., California

A gloomy day turns into a sunny one.

Deborah wrote to me of the day that her car broke down on the freeway. Here is her story in her own words:

"I am in the fast lane with a dead car surrounded by anxious, frantic, and aggressive drivers heading to their workplaces. I have no one to call and ask for help; I have no "roadside service" in my insurance plan, and I can't call anyone anyway because the phones are on the other side of the freeway. The cars continue to whiz by me and the freeway becomes more jammed by the minute. The fumes from the exhaust begin to make me weary as I stare at the multitude of red taillights now creating a four-dimensional kind f red-domino effect.

Wait! What's this? Red and yellow lights behind me...a tow truck! A very large, well-built and well-groomed young man dressed in rain gear approaches. He immediately identifies himself. He is not a mechanic, but will try to get the car started. He works for the Department of Transportation, he says. If he cannot get the car to start, he will tow the car to a safe place where I can call someone. He tells me that he cannot take it to a specific repair shop, but he will get me someplace where I will have several choices, and I will be safe and comfortable and can make phone calls. And, he is going to do all of this at no charge.

He ultimately tows my crippled vehicle since it wouldn't start, and I am taken in his lovely truck to a safe haven. He is my angel of the freeway, a knight not in shining armor, but shiny new rain gear. His hands are clean, he is nice, patient, and drives very carefully. As he drops off my car, and I step out of his big, white truck, he drives off into the rain. I smile to myself that what started out as such a gloomy day turned into a sunny one."

Marcia R., Arizona, Manager of Staff Development

A young girl's long journey is made safer by extraordinary help.

"I managed to screw up my life royally when I was young even though I was the kind of person you'd think of as the all-American "girl-next-door". I got into trouble with a heroin addiction when I was 20 years old and was forced to go into a court-ordered drug rehabilitation program in Las Vegas. It felt strange at the beginning to be the only Caucasian person in the program, so I was already an outsider, and although I wanted to take classes, they would only allow me to study how to change oil in a car. I didn't relate well to the treatment methodology either (called attack therapy) which is very harsh and demeaning. It's interesting to note that not long after the time we are talking about here, that treatment mode itself came under critical scrutiny and was phased out as ineffective.

I managed to stick it out for six months before I snapped one weekend and became hysterical. My only choice, I felt, was to escape. I had a change of clothes in a bag in my room, and exactly one dime to my name when I left by the back door. I found myself wandering aimlessly through the neighborhood the clinic was located in and feeling cold, scared, and directionless. The only thing I knew for sure was that I needed to get back to Phoenix.

At the end of one of the many alleys I roamed, was an idling car driven by a huge black woman who told me curtly to "Get in." Thankful for anything that got me off my feet, off the street, and away from feeling so alone, I climbed in only to find myself driven to the house of a man who gave the woman some money, which immediately made me very nervous. He said to me, "Would you like to go out?" Instantly I agreed since I would be among other people which might be safer than where I was now, and might afford me the chance to escape. I began making silent pleas to God to get me safely out of this situation.

In the car, the man asked, "Is there anything I can do for you?" Taking him at his word, I replied, "You can buy me a bus ticket to Phoenix", which surprisingly, he did.

We went to some kind of lounge, where I used the phone to call my mother with the following message: "Don't ask any questions. I'll be there in the morning and I need you to find a lawyer to go to the probation office with me because I am NOT coming back to this program." It was now 11:00 p.m. and my bus would leave at 2 a.m. I sat with the man for a while in the bar, then helped get him back to his house where he passed out. I took the bus ticket and 50 cents for the phone off his table and left.

When we were out previously, I had paid attention to the route to the bus station, so I headed straight there. I stopped in confusion a little way from the station because I was afraid to continue--there were several police officers in view. I didn't know if this was normal or out of the ordinary. Suddenly a man materialized behind me and said, "What is there to do in this town besides gamble?" He clearly was not a local. I looked at him, "Where are you from?" He replied, "I'm from San Diego, but I'm going back through Phoenix in the morning." This was a godsend. Perhaps I had another way to get home besides the bus because the station was looking less promising with each passing minute.

I asked him if I could ride with him and he was open to that so we went together to his hotel so I could rest. My new friend went out to gamble, but came back a short time later and said, "Why don't we just leave now?" We did, and I found this man from Jamaica to be an interesting traveling companion who was good to me by taking me right to my parents' house. I later went with my mother and a lawyer to the probation office before they called from Las Vegas. I was very fortunate there also, in that they didn't put me in jail for violating the court order but instead gave me a second chance.

In this situation, I felt I was protected constantly from all kinds of weird circumstances where I could have been harmed. I wasn't really afraid, because I knew I wasn't alone. Many times in my life I have been in danger: accidents where cars have been totaled, overdoses from drugs, and once being left for dead in the back room of a hospital. But I always knew I was being protected and helped.

Ultimately, my life has turned around. I healed the damaged relationship with my parents, went to school and obtained two masters degrees, achieved a responsible management position in a high-tech organization, and authored three books of both fiction and non-fiction. I believe I was g<u>uided</u> to do all of this, because I know that left to flounder in my own weaknesses, I would have ended up in the gutter."

Kelley B., California, Human Resources

A stranger helps renew the will to live.

"I know that I was comforted in a very special way during an immensely difficult time in my life. When my youngest child was born (these kids are now 9, 8, and 5), I became deeply depressed because my children were sick all the time, and I was alone since my husband was stationed in the Persian Gulf. One day, a friend took my kids so I could get a break and I drove my Bronco toward the cliffs overlooking Palos Verde/San Pedro. I was considering just driving my car right over the cliff because I didn't care at that moment if I lived or died.

As this thought was taking shape, I paused for a minute and got a vision of what it would be like for my kids to grow up without a mother and that made me wait long enough to rethink it. At that second, a man walked up to me and started asking me about my truck. We just started talking and went on and on for the longest time. The more we talked, the more I calmed down and realized that there was a lot to live for. By the time we said goodbye, I was feeling much better and had kind of a renewed lease on my life. I asked him why he spoke to me--did he really want to know about the Bronco? This kind man just smiled mysteriously and said, "You looked like you needed to talk."

He told me that if I ever needed a friend to talk again, that he came to the cliffs on Tuesday and Thursday from 11:00 to 1:00. But it was very strange--although I went several times to look for him when he said he would be there, I never did see him again. It felt like I had lost a friend and yet I had only spoken to this man one time. Maybe because of the intensity of our one long talk, I had stronger feelings than I would have otherwise. When I think about it now, I wonder if maybe he was only meant to be in that place and time the day I needed my life to be saved? Even if this was just a human being that protected me somehow, God had given me another chance."

Jane M, Arizona, Consultant

A fun day trip turns ominous for a stranded mom and kids.

"I'd finally decided to have a trip to see snow with the kids. There had been significant snowfall in northern Arizona, so I headed off with my two boys and their two best friends. We played in the snow for a long time, and then as it started to snow heavily, the traffic on the nearby road became noticeably lighter. I began to get nervous and decided I better leave with the kids before it got dark. When we tried to pull out, we realized our vehicle was completely embedded in snow. We had not realized the depth of the snow when we left the road. I tried everything to move that vehicle forward. I put jackets under the tires. I asked the kids to help push where they could. Nothing would budge that vehicle. We didn't have cell phones at that time, and my husband didn't know exactly where I was. After 90 minutes with no success and no cars passing by that could be signaled for help, it started to get dark. And I started to feel panic rising up. Suddenly, a man in a truck appeared on the road and stopped. It seemed as if he was headed directly toward me rather than simply driving past. And he had a hitch on that truck! To my enormous relief, he pulled us out and I continued to call him my "snow angel" for many years."

Reflect and Act

Reflect:

- When you are in a situation to be able to help someone, what makes you <u>CHOOSE</u> to help rather than just being an observer?
- How often do you recognize that help you receive—or that something appearing in your life—might be guided by divine timing, rather than just chance?
- Do you recall a recent opportunity where you could help someone, but you did not actively choose to engage? What led to that decision?
- How could you be more aware of the generosity of spirit in others, seeing them as instruments of God's love and guidance in your life?

Act:

- Take a moment at the end of the day to think about if you missed opportunities, or if you stepped in when God placed you "in the right place at the right time."

- How can you actively cultivate a mindset that allows you to act as an instrument of God's love, stepping in to help others even when it is unexpected or requires extra effort?
- In the future, watch for a specific opportunity to offer your help to someone the next time they express a need for help, or when you see a situation where you could step in.
- What steps can you take to be more present and attentive in daily life so that, like the helpers in these stories, you can recognize opportunities to assist others at precisely the right moment?

3

GOD HELPS THOSE WHO HELP OTHERS

A true expression of altruistic love is the willingness to help other people. We all have the ability to become "earth angels" or instruments of God here on earth in service to our fellow humans. There is a great joy in giving to other people whether in crisis circumstances or just in the living of an ordinary day. In the examples in the following pages, you will see someone in the right place at the right time for handling an emergency, as when Bob was almost decapitated in an army tank, Karen's aunt was on the verge of suicide, or Keri Lee's stepfather was on the verge of a coma. Each of them at one specific moment in time either needed someone else to be there for them or were the ones to offer a gift of life.

Not all circumstances are as dramatic as these. Sometimes, the ability to touch the heart of a relative, friend, or acquaintance makes all the difference in the world. And some give themselves in service every day such as the people portrayed in the stories of the Make-a-Wish Foundation.

As you read these, offer a prayer that you can be open to being an instrument of God, and that you will look for ways to be there to help others.

Bob R., Arizona, Personnel Analyst

The unexpected rotation of an army tank turret threatens to decapitate a young soldier!

Bob's experience with a near-fatal tank accident while in the army led him to believe that he was "particularly graced in a moment of danger", and there was no chance that it was mere coincidence that saved him. Bob's job at a Kentucky army base required him to be a tank driver occupying the position in the front part of the tank. One day, as he pulled himself up to leave his station to go into the turret, suddenly it began to swivel because the tank commander at the controls (who cannot see the driver's position) had not checked where Bob was before initiating the rotation.

To leave the narrow driver's position, he had to pull himself upwards and backwards from a bucket-like seat using two rails, one on either side of his head. As he felt the turret begin to move, Bob was faced with a terrible choice as a huge metal brace on the inside of the turret came toward him--continue to pull himself up but probably have both his legs cut off since there wasn't enough time to exit, or try to drop back down and risk being decapitated. He made the split-second choice to drop down.

"Although there was only a fleeting moment involved, I actually thought about missing my family, and how ironic it was that I had avoided being sent to Vietnam only to die at home in the USA on a routine maneuver. As the brace crossed my chest, crushing it, I lost consciousness. My next memory was waking up with my fellow crew members around looking down at me, and discovering what a miracle had happened.

Here's what I didn't know...at the last possible second, one of the other two people in the tank besides the commander and me had seen what was about to happen and had grabbed the tank commander's leg and pulled it hard enough to get him to stop what he was doing. The odd thing was that the guy who saw me and managed to help shouldn't have been in that position at that moment, and it was truly unusual that he happened to be there.

I could hardly believe it: I wasn't cut in half, I wasn't dead, I was fine. In fact, I didn't even have any injuries except for having had the breath knocked out of me. No way should that have happened the way it did...but I do not think it was some kind of lucky coincidence; it was an instant of Grace for which I have been thankful ever since."

Pam C., Louisiana, Medical Office Management

A lost brother comes back to his family.

"I want to tell how my family miraculously found my missing brother even though we had no leads, no information, and were being stymied by the public service people who could have given us help.

My brother Karl, a very talented artist who has shown his work both nationally and locally, was living in San Diego although the rest of the family lived in Louisiana. We all contacted him for Easter that year, but he didn't return any messages, which created a warning flag for the whole family. And then his employer called to find out if he had spent the holiday with the family and when would he be returning? Big red flag!

We found out later that for the week following that April 25 Easter day, his landlord, his neighbor, and a good friend were also conducting a search. The neighbor had been alerted that his faithful Weimaraner "Kehma," who was the love of his life, was not being cared for when the dog howled continuously. A check by the landlord revealed the dog was alone in an apartment where she had torn apart an unopened bag of dog food and was drinking from the toilet. Karl would never let that happen.

My brother's friend, Bill, discovered that Karl had been arrested by the San Diego police for drunk driving early on that Easter morning. But he didn't drink! In fact, Bill had encouraged him to make an appointment with the doctor for right after Easter to find out where his dizzy spells and forgetfulness were coming from. When Bill talked to the police station, he was told there was something physically wrong with Karl and some tests needed to be run. They didn't allow him to talk to Karl, and further calls only revealed that he had been released. That was the last trace of him.

By now frantic, I tried to help my family do some long-distance searching. I assured the police that Karl would never leave his beloved Kehma, and would never keep his family in the dark as to his whereabouts. Only two years earlier, both a father and sister died of cancer and he knew that my mother and the rest of us couldn't handle another loss. I filed a missing person report, but the police said that even if they knew where he was they couldn't tell me; I checked the morgue daily; I called the five hospitals they gave me numbers for and my brother was not registered as a patient at any of them.

From the jail, I could obtain only the following information: Karl had been tested for drugs and alcohol and the results were negative, so he had been "released onto the street from the jail." Bill told us Karl seemed to be suffering from some ailment that caused amnesia-like symptoms, which only worried us more. Was he wandering the streets of San Diego not knowing who he was, or where home was? These questions swam through our minds back in Louisiana.

Finally, after twelve days with no new information, my husband and I left for the West Coast to do more intensive investigation. We decided to drive in case we didn't find Karl because we would have to pack up his apartment where the rent was now overdue, and retrieve Kehma from the county animal shelter where she was in protective custody from being abandoned. My younger sister and her husband moved into our home to care for our three children, and we drove mile after mile praying constantly and strategizing so that once we arrived, we wouldn't waste a minute.

We arrived on May 3 and got to work. On the answering machine in Karl's apartment, among the desperate messages from the family, were interspersed calls from various friends who left their own numbers for a return call. We checked each one for any kind of lead. Nothing. I had made up flyers with a recent picture. Nothing. We went from floor to floor questioning nurses at the two hospitals that took patients who did not have health insurance, since that was true of Karl. Nothing. We met with a representative from the Missing Persons Division and found out Karl had been released wearing "an orange shirt and blue jeans." But nothing else. We searched the two major homeless shelters (for someone from a small southern town, I must have seemed rather naive. I had no idea that so many homeless individuals existed). Still nothing. The Salvation Army shelter told us that even if he was staying there, they wouldn't be able to tell us. We were told we could return the following morning and check the faces of the several hundred people who lined up for breakfast. Nothing. We drove the streets of San Diego for four hours crisscrossing a twelve-block area where homeless people wander. And still nothing. We were frustrated and despairing.

That night one more bit of grim news...the police called and said that Karl's vehicle, the one driven when he had been arrested, was impounded at a wrecker yard and the various fees now exceeded the value of the car.

Finally, Bill suggested trying the television stations to see if we could get the word out on a mass scale. Channel 3 (God bless them!) was very interested and conducted a detailed interview where I pleaded for help from the people of San Diego. They showed Karl's picture and gave two numbers: the Missing Persons Department, and my mother's home to call collect. The story aired at 5:00, 6:00, and 10:00 on their news shows. Interestingly enough, another major station took some notes for a brief story, which I am not aware that ever aired, and the third station was not interested at all. So, we had only <u>one</u> chance.

That night my mother called us–Karl had contacted her because of the news story. How fortunate that he was tuned into the one station willing to put on this story at exactly the time it aired. Or maybe he was receiving a little Divine help? He was suffering from a form of dementia that had him living in a kind of fantasy, not knowing where he was or where he had been from one moment to the next. He had seen his face and mine on the screen and had called the number. He thought he was in Lafayette next door to my mother. She kept him on the line for an hour and the police were summoned to trace the call. A nurse eventually came into the room, but said she couldn't tell my mother where Karl was calling from. When the police got on the line and said that his family had driven cross-country to find him, she finally revealed the name of the small private hospital where he was. Although we had called there previously and been told he wasn't a patient, we were overjoyed and drove to the facility immediately, arriving well after 11:00 when Karl was sleeping.

We spent the next day sorting out details with the hospital and getting ready to take Karl with us back to Louisiana because he was in no shape to be left on his own–doctors were pessimistic about his condition. The doctors were angry with the police who had released him from arrest at the door to the emergency room. They had taken him to the facility that treats their inmates, but had not admitted him while in their custody because they would then be responsible for payment. The police thought he was ill because he was clearly incapacitated but not under the influence of any substances.

The hospital discharged him to our care two days later, the day after his thirty-first birthday, and there wasn't a dry eye as he was reunited with one of the few things he recognized–his beloved Kehma. We started the long journey home with an invalid who could not walk, feed himself, go to the bathroom on his own, or care for his pet. We had as much of his life as we could fit into the trailer, and we drove for 72 hours. We arrived in my mother's driveway on Mother's Day...what better gift for a worried mom?

After two more years of ups and downs, Karl died peacefully at the University Medical Center, almost two years to the day since we had brought him home.

Something very interesting happened after his death. When I wanted to feel closer to Karl, I would visit a local art store that had one of his prints for sale. There was no way I could afford what they were asking, so I would just look at it and talk silently to him and feel a little better for being close to a part of him. I would ask Karl through prayer to let me know that he was happy and had not forgotten me.

One day to my surprise when I visited the store, the print was on the framing table being prepared for a customer. I asked the clerk who was purchasing it and she pointed to a lady on the other side of the store. I was shocked to see the mother of a friend of my daughter, and she was surprised to see me. She told me she had chosen the print because it was perfect for her newly remodeled kitchen, but as I passed my fingers lightly and lovingly over Karl's signature, she said she hadn't looked at the artist's name. She was astonished to see Karl's name and told me that she knew him from the Artists' Alliance and was thrilled to have one of his pieces. The print took on a new and added meaning for her.

I was delighted that it was going to "a good home" and I might even have a chance to visit it from time to time. We both had a good cry right there in the store with feelings both happy and sad. Although the feeling was probably stronger for me, we both believed that my brother was letting us know that he hadn't forgotten us."

Keri Lee P., California

An insistent inner voice sends Keri Lee racing to her stepfather's side.

"I want to describe an experience I have never forgotten! One evening, I felt a very strong inner urging to call my former stepfather. I adored this man, but hesitated to call him frequently. He and my mother had divorced five years earlier and he had a serious drinking problem. When I called, he tended to keep me on the phone for a really long time, and I would eventually become irritated at his feelings of self-pity. I felt that urge to call him and pushed it aside although I did tell my newlywed husband about the inner prompting. Back it came, even stronger! A second time I mentioned it to my husband as I was pushing it away, and he said I really should call then. But no, I again disregarded the feeling.

Within the next few minutes, I felt the strongest urging of all, the equivalent of someone grabbing me by "inner shoulders and shaking me," and it felt like a silent voice <u>screaming</u> at me saying "Get up and call him <u>NOW!</u>" This felt so weird and so insistent that I did indeed call my stepfather right at that moment.

He answered the phone, gasped and stuttered and then apparently dropped the receiver. I yelled at him repeatedly to pick the phone up. My husband, who heard me screaming, instantly became as concerned as I was and insisted that we go to my stepfather's house immediately. With my heart racing the entire time, we drove the 20 miles to his house well above the speed limit. We found my stepfather shaking and disoriented, unable to speak to us. He could only manage a halting stutter. Deeply worried, we called 911 and he went by ambulance to the hospital. By the time we arrived at the ER, he was experiencing seizures and he ended up in a semi-coma state for almost two weeks.

We later discovered that missionaries from our church had challenged him to quit drinking, and he had abruptly stopped putting alcohol into his system. The sudden withdrawal was affecting his body quite severely. We were told that if he had not gotten to the hospital and been treated when he did, it was very likely he would have died.

This story had a bittersweet ending. My stepfather and my mother remarried when he was sober, and he never touched a drop of alcohol after that. However, he was a 22-year veteran state police officer and died in 1995 from cancer caused by exposure to asbestos, rather than anything related to his drinking.

My husband and I always felt that it was divine intervention that caused us to call him that night. I am so glad I finally listened to the promptings I was receiving and did not ignore the way God was trying to use me."

Karen B., Birmingham, England, Receptionist

A young woman is guided to help her despairing aunt.

"I had a most extraordinary experience while I was ironing one time. I distinctly heard my name called out, "Karen!" It sounded like my mother's voice, but she had been dead for several years. My mother's voice was very similar to my aunt's, and I had a sudden, overwhelming urge to call my aunt, which I did. She said to me, "Why did you call?" "I don't know", I replied, "But I think you need me."

She then somewhat ashamedly told me that she was standing there at that very moment with pills in her hand ready to take her own life. I tried very hard to calm her down and keep her talking to distract her from her deadly intention. She was in a very bad emotional state. She had gotten involved with the wrong person against everyone's advice, and had been suffering from severe mental and physical abuse. This had been going on for a long time without her letting anyone know about it. She was in terrible emotional pain and couldn't see any other way out.

I finally talked her out of suicide and got her willing to consider other alternatives. I am so glad that I paid attention to that voice calling my name. I don't know what it was, but something was definitely guiding me in helping my aunt."

Alma F., California, Import/Export Clerk

Alma's gift touches the heart of her teacher.

"I was attending night school to get a typing certificate, and I felt that I wanted to express my appreciation to my teacher for what I had learned. Why not take some nice flowers to her, I thought? At the floral shop, I began to have second thoughts as I looked at the flowers, fearing that maybe she would think I was trying to bribe her for a good grade or something.

Instead, I saw a nice candy rose made out of white chocolate and decided to bring this instead. When I shyly presented this to my teacher after class and said thanks for her help, she surprised me by bursting into tears and hugging me.

My teacher told me that she had been saying a novena to St. Therese of Lisieux and this was the last day of that novena. In the novena prayer there was a line something about "A white rose is a sign of Your Love..." (St. Therese is often pictured holding white flowers). My teacher said that she felt that this was a message to her that her prayer had been heard."

Three wonderful stories about the people who serve children through the Make-A-Wish foundation were shared with me when I participated in a Texas conference.

Susie V., Oklahoma, Oklahoma Wish Coordinator

Susie helps fulfill a child's dream.

So strongly does Susie feel her purpose is to serve at Make-A-Wish, that she gave up her focus on a law career to do it. She was working on a wish that had desperate urgency. The two-year old "wish child" was expected to live for little more than a month since the doctors had already stopped treatments. He had chosen a visit with Barney as his number one wish, and a visit with Sesame Street characters as number two. The visit with Barney required several children to participate and she wasn't working with any other children in this timeframe. Sesame Street Park wouldn't open until May and her child wouldn't make it that far.

Susie sat at her desk agonizing over how to best help this child since the social workers were pressuring her to hurry. The phone rang. A producer from the Sesame Street Road Tour said that the tour would be in town on a certain date a month later, and did Make-A-Wish have any children they would want to have visit? Susie was ecstatic at being able to provide Travis the one thing that would cheer him. Travis indeed did go to the production arena, and was the only child participating in that personal visit. He gave everyone such joy that day as he laughed and giggled with delight—something he hadn't done in months!

Terri B., Virginia

Terri sees impossible airline reservations happen.

Terri can think of several times that the most unusual circumstances affected wishes her chapter was granting. An older wish-child had just requested a computer setup, the first one in 18 months. The new Executive Director was deciding what to do when a stranger walked into the office. "Hi, I'm Rusty and I've done volunteering on wishes in the past. Do you need anybody right now to do some computer work?" The Executive Director was delighted—here was the very person she needed. Rusty not only took care of that wish but has been helping out since, doing interesting things to customize the programs and put in "bells and whistles" applicable to each different child.

Terri was new to her job, having been there only three months, when a wish came in to meet Shaquille O'Neal. Terri was typing the paperwork at the very moment a fax appeared on their machine.

The new (one-month-old) Orlando Make-A-Wish chapter was distributing the guidelines they had established for any wishes to meet Shaq. They had set up some procedures because they had begun to receive so many requests from around the country. There were five open dates! Terri began to make the airline reservations for the seven family members but discovered that their preferred date was during spring break, and she couldn't find any open seats. The reservation agent, Chris, had just said there were no seats when he placed her on hold to assist on something else for a moment. When he returned to the line, he went back into the computer to try to find the next best option. Suddenly, he found that seven seats had opened on the exact flight she needed. He seemed to think that this was extremely unusual. Terri was thrilled to be able to fulfill the wish after all, just as the child had wanted.

Dottie R., North Carolina, Executive Director

Dottie's volunteering becomes a career.

Dottie is well-known for her dedication to people. The editors of her yearbook had written about her, "The joy of her life is serving others." For years, Dottie had volunteered at hospitals, for the Red Cross etc. After seeing a newspaper story about a wish child, Dottie thought that Make-A-Wish could certainly use her skills and talents. She had made a few phone calls to inquire, but had been unsuccessful so far. Frustrated, she wasn't sure where to look next when across her TV came a "trailer." Dottie was surprised to see that the advertisement trailer (probably a PSA or Public Service Announcement) gave a number to call to volunteer for Make-A-Wish. Dottie immediately followed up on that information, first volunteering and then later becoming the Executive Director when the position opened up. Dottie was perfect for the job—and no one else even applied.

Kathy S., New Mexico, Banking

A family gift returns in an unusual way.

"This may not seem like a very big thing, but I thought it was quite curious. At Christmastime one year, I knew that my sister who is very poor and has six kids was desperate and struggling to provide any kind of holiday at all for her family. I had stopped at her house on my way to the mall and the $50 in my pocket was earmarked for a particular item. Impulsively, I reached in my pocket, pulled it out and gave it to her, asking her not to say anything about it to anyone, but just use it wherever she could to do something a little extra for her family.

She was very appreciative, but the oddest thing happened the following month. I entered the Superbowl "pool" at work, and despite never having participated before, I won $50, exactly the amount I had given my sister. Could it be just a coincidence? It certainly could, except I felt that maybe it was in recognition for what I had given away."

Anne K., Massachusetts, Registered Nurse

The priest who is needed returns mysteriously.

"In our hospital, a child under our care took a turn for the worse. The mother asked if a priest was available to be with the child. Although she wasn't a Catholic, it was important to her that a "religious" presence be there while she was so distraught.

We did have a priest who had come that morning and had been visiting several patients, but no one on the staff was sure where he had gone. We didn't have a number to contact him, but the woman was insistent that someone be there. Since I knew that the priest had finished his rounds and had probably left the hospital, I stood for a moment in frustration thinking "What could I do now to help her?" At that moment, the very man I needed walked around the corner. I believe that he was sent back to us as an answer to a frantic prayer."

Kristi K., Michigan, Medical Field

Kristi's overpowering urge to see a friend guides her to the scene of an accident involving that friend.

Kristi was shopping at a favorite farmer's market for some fresh, new sweet corn. She was holding several ears that she planned to purchase, when suddenly she felt she simply must see a friend who worked on the other side of town.

This feeling was so overpowering that the corn fell from her hands and she ran to her car and drove immediately to her friend's office. Kristi was a little chagrined to discover that her friend wasn't even working that day and concluded that she had somehow become confused and gotten carried away in her thoughts. So, she spent a short time talking with the people at the office who worked with her friend, and then decided to return and finish her shopping.

As she reached the driveway, she inexplicably turned to the right instead of the left which would have returned her to the market the exact way she had come. The right turn was a less convenient way to go, and Kristi was surprised she had done this. At the very next intersection, she discovered her friend on the ground at the scene of an accident; her friend had been hit by another car and was injured.

Kristi's friend was in pain but conscious and amazed to see her, and tremendously appreciated her support and presence. Kristi did not feel that she could have done anything to avert the accident, but believed that the guiding hand which had sent her there meant for her to comfort her friend at a difficult time.

Suzi L., California, Administrative Assistant

Suzi appears to be the only hope for her best friend.

Suzi's story is a remarkable testament to the courage and strength of one person who was given the love and support of human friends. Suzi had a long-time friendship with a woman that had started in the fourth grade. Her friend was in a terrible accident and sustained life-threatening injuries because she was not wearing a seat belt. The friend ended up in the hospital in a deep coma and did not respond to anything but the sound of Suzi's voice talking about very ordinary, everyday incidents. Each time Suzi visited, the nursing staff saw a change in the friend's heart rate and brain waves on the monitors they watched, and asked Suzi to come periodically to stimulate her. Although it seemed like an impossibility, some believed that the friend would ultimately awaken, especially Suzi, who conveyed this calm certainty at each visit.

The coma lasted an astonishing six months, but the friend did finally regain consciousness and immediately recognized Suzi, who was ecstatic. The friend who was not supposed to live, much less walk again and function with any degree of normality, made consistent progress.

Suzi said, "My friend improved over a two-year period and slowly learned to walk, talk, and read again. About 2 1/2 years after her accident, my friend fulfilled a 20-year- old promise and acted as the maid of honor at my wedding. I couldn't have been happier. Today my friend functions fairly well although she cannot live alone; but she does improve all the time with her walking, talking, reading, and writing. I admire her courage so much because of the incredible difficulties she has faced and the grace with which she manages every day of her life. I'm not sure anyone else could be as strong. She is a role model for me as well as for everyone else who knows her, and so maybe fulfills some kind of purpose in her life to inspire others."

Dawn A., Arizona, Clerk

A good friend with an unusually strong psychic bond offers emotional support.

"I have the most unusual connection to a very dear friend whom I have known since junior high school. If anything bad happens to me, Shanie seems to know. Whether she is nearby or in a different state, she knows exactly what's going on with me. One time I awoke with half of my face paralyzed and doctors kept me for a whole day testing for everything including a brain tumor. By the time I returned home, there were three messages from Shanie and she was crying on the third one. She knew I was in trouble. Everything did turn out alright that time, however.

Another time, I was in a car accident in early December and received no serious injuries although I was badly shaken up. My car, however, was a total loss.

The next morning, very early, Shanie was on my phone. She had had a dream that I was hurt and wanted to call in the middle of the night. Her husband made her wait until the next morning, but of course, she knew something wasn't right with me. Our bond is so strong that we will probably always be aware of what is happening in each other's lives."

Reflect and Act

Reflect

- How often do you see yourself as a potential "earth angel," and are there any ways you might be overlooking opportunities to serve as an instrument of God in the lives of others?
- When you did act to help someone in need because you were in the right place, did some unexpected resource appear that assisted you with the support you were offering or allowed you to accomplish what the other person needed?
- Were there times you didn't assist because you didn't think you had the capability?
- Do you recall a time when you experienced joy, connection, or meaning from helping someone else, and how does that reflect God working through you in the lives of others?

Act

- If you see an opportunity to step in and act as an "earth angel" for someone, don't doubt the guidance you are getting and just take act. Believe that God will send whatever support you need.

- Decide what intentional practices such as prayer, mindfulness, or presence can help you become more open to recognizing moments when you can act as God's instrument to help someone in need.
- Make a habit of offering small acts of service or kindness every day, so that you are consistently aligned with the divine flow of helping others and being available at critical moments.

4

THE CHILDREN ARE ALWAYS PROTECTED

Children are especially well-loved by God and His angels as several Bible passages mention. One of the most famous pictures of a "guardian" angel is the one where two small children are crossing a bridge and a watchful angel hovers behind them. Anyone familiar with that picture will recognize the spirit of loving care that it represents. Following are inspiring stories where children are protected in extremely unusual but important ways.

Pam S., Ohio, Teacher

A baby in a stroller is saved from plunging off a pier.

"I was on a pier at Lake Erie with my youngest son strapped into a stroller, and I thought the brakes on the wheels were securely locked so I wasn't concerned about being on the pier. Suddenly I looked up and realized that the stroller was rolling away from me and I ran after it, absolutely petrified with fear as it approached the edge of the dock. The stroller stopped abruptly as the back wheels were right at the very edge of the pier, and I was able to reach out and grab it with shaking hands. At that place, the pier is about 10-12 feet above the waterline, and the water is deep because ships dock there.

The thought that my son was one second away from plunging into water was horrifying because he would have sunk too fast for me to save him. That child is very special to us. My husband and I were told that we would be unable to have children and after that we had two, so we feel extremely blessed. I know that something was protecting my child the day that I have described."

Jeana L., California, Real Estate

A two-year-old miraculously heals from a fireworks injury to the consternation of his examining doctor.

"At a block party on our street, it got a little wild and some of the kids as well as the adults were playing with bottle rockets. I was there with my two-year old son, and so I decided to leave because I thought it might be a getting a little dangerous. All of a sudden, one of the bottle rockets whizzed past my son's face blistering and burning it, as well as severely injuring his eye. It looked awful and I was terrified.

I raced him to the hospital, and we went into the emergency room where he was briefly examined before we were asked to fill out some paperwork because they had decided to admit him for treatment and observation. It took maybe fifteen minutes to do this paperwork. Eventually the doctor came back to treat my son, and a miracle had occurred. There was no more blistering or redness, and no damage to his eye. All signs of the injury had completely disappeared, and the doctor asked me where the other child was, thinking this was not my son. He said, "This can't be the child I looked at a few minutes ago." I assured him that it was. He told me, "This child is fine; go ahead and take him home, because there is no problem. But I haven't seen anything like this before." I was amazed, confused, happy, and disbelieving all at the same time, because I had seen how terrible the burns and redness were, and my son was just as good as new!"

Deanna S., Florida, Executive Secretary/Medical

Deanna's baby is protected in a most unusual way.

"I was living in Portland on campus at the University. I remember walking to my apartment one time carrying my four-month-old daughter, Jamie, in a kind of pouch or pack in front of me. The weather wasn't the best since it was December. As I crossed the street, I tried to step up onto the curb not realizing that it was a higher curb than normal. I tripped and began to fall right onto the baby I carried; there wasn't even time to put my arms out to try and break the fall or protect the child. The next thing I knew, I was on my back with my body cushioning the baby who now laid on top of me like she was lying on a big pillow. I have absolutely no idea how I could have flipped myself over when I didn't even have time to start to react.

To this day, I believe that God or one of His angels was right there beside me and flipped me over to protect the baby. Jamie is a most exceptional child. She even survived an attack of encephalitis at the age of nine, and I think God must have some very special plans in mind for her."

Lorie B., Arizona

A young mother is shown where two terrified little boys are trapped just in time to save them.

"I was babysitting my nephew and my son one summer day in the Midwest, and the kids were playing happily in the fenced backyard. I had gone into the house for just a minute to get the boys something to drink, figuring they were perfectly safe since there was no way they could get out of the enclosure. Suddenly, I heard my nephew "Joey" crying pitifully, and ran outside, looking frantically behind the garage, into every corner, around to the front, and I just couldn't see anything. Where had they gone?

I did not hear my own son, "Bobby," only the continual but steadily fainter cries from Joey. The gate was closed and I stood in confusion on the back porch not knowing where else to look, staring into the frustratingly empty yard.

Suddenly, I found myself with my hand on the door of an old, unused refrigerator on the porch, which had been behind me since I had been facing out into the yard. Almost like awakening from a trance, I shook my head to clear it, pulled open the door, and discovered the terrified boys stuffed inside.

I know it seems obvious after the fact to check the refrigerator, but at the time it was the farthest thing from my mind, and I am not convinced I would have thought of it in time on my own. If the boys had fainted, they would have suffocated while I searched all the other parts of the backyard. I have never told my family this in all these years because I didn't want my sister to know that I had unintentionally allowed her son to be in such danger. I know that if anything had happened to the boys, I would never have recovered from the guilt. To this day, it gives me a cold sweat to talk about what a close call they had, and I am forever grateful to whatever angel put my hand on that door."

Cheri C., Washington, Retail Sales

Two young girls are protected from serious harm.

"I definitely believe in divine intervention. When I was living in Okinawa, I was driving one time on a rain-slicked road near a small Japanese school. There was a lot of traffic and the area was extremely congested with pedestrians. Suddenly, two young girls darted out in front of my car–and I realized with horror that I probably couldn't stop quickly enough. I slammed on my brakes and slid on the wet pavement certain that I would hit one or both. As I came to a stop, the skirt of one of the girls just brushed the bumper–something that seemed impossible! It was like an invisible hand came out, blocked my car and gave the young ladies a gentle push. I knew something unusual had happened there."

Dennie B., Oklahoma, Environmental Consulting

How did the father of the drowning boy appear at just the right moment?

"My three sons are very close in age. Many years ago, when they were little, we had a most frightening thing happen. The youngest, Greg, was just six years old and the middle son,

Scott, was eight when the "boat dock incident" almost changed our lives.

On this day, the boys and I were lounging on the pontoon boat as it was tied up at the dock, and they were playing while I read. Suddenly Scott pushed the youngest one, Greg, into the deep, dark water. I was terrified because I am afraid of the water and Scott was probably not strong enough to rescue his brother. I was not sure that Greg was going to be able to swim to safety because he was scared to death and thrashing wildly.

All at once, my husband Doug came walking unexpectedly toward the dock dressed in his business suit and carrying his briefcase. I screamed hysterically at him that Greg was in the water, and he jumped in suit, shoes, and all, to rescue our son. Doug says he had been compelled to come home early from work that day and had driven to the dock not even knowing we were there. He said he was puzzled about why he had felt such a strong urging to drive down to the boat.

Could it really just have been a coincidence that he had happened to arrive at the place where we were, exactly at the moment that our son was in danger? Probably not. We feel that he had been inspired to be there to save Greg's life. Greg could very well have drowned that day and that would have altered our family's life forever."

Marilyn T., Minnesota, Insurance

Unusual timing on a daughter's death.

Marilyn experienced an interesting coincidence at the time of her daughter's death. Her baby was only 3 and 1/2 years old when she had to have open heart surgery early in November for a congenital heart defect.

"She was in the Intensive Care Unit on Christmas Eve, but didn't seem to want me there with her. She was quite lethargic and kept turning away, so it seemed futile to stay. Instead, I went home and spent Christmas Eve with my son so he could have the best holiday possible under the circumstances.

I went back for part of Christmas Day and was with her when she died the day after Christmas. Our family always thought that she had waited somehow until after the holiday, because the memory of a death on Christmas Day would always make that a very sad day forever after. It could easily just have been a coincidence, but I like to think that maybe there was a purpose to how things turned out."

Barb B., Arizona, Community College Personnel

Barb and a friend experience an odd coincidence...were they saved from becoming the first victims of serial killer Ted Bundy?

"My story is one of those weird coincidences that makes you stop and say, "I wonder if..." It is about a potential encounter with a serial killer named Ted Bundy, who was executed for his crimes in 1989.

When I was 14 years old, I was living in a house on Lake Sammamish in Washington state with my mother, and the state park was about two miles down the road. My friends and I routinely rode there on our bikes, spending a lot of our non-school time at the park sunbathing or just hanging out. One afternoon, a friend and I started out for the park, but for some reason turned around and didn't go. I don't remember now what it was that turned us back, maybe a flat tire on the bike or maybe we had forgotten something...

At the time, we were glad we hadn't been at the park that day because a young girl was abducted that very afternoon, right at the same time we would have been there. Much later we discovered that she had been Ted Bundy's first victim in his killing spree. We both fit the profile of his victims that was developed later--long brown hair, young, slender...Might it have been one of us instead? Of course, we'll never know, but it does make you wonder if somehow we had been protected from potential harm."

Renee J., Arizona, Business Manager

A helpful nurse may have been a guardian angel.

"When I was around 5 years old, I had to stay overnight in a hospital because of a severe infection. I was terribly unhappy when my parents left and cried uncontrollably because I didn't want to be alone in that big, strange place. My parents had looked so sad to say goodbye to me, so I knew they didn't want me there either.

Shortly after that, while I was still sobbing hysterically, a nice, pretty nurse came to see me. She said her name was Mary Ann, and she had lovely black hair and was dressed in white. She told me that she would take special care of me so that I wouldn't be afraid.

Mary Ann made me laugh and I felt so good, not crying anymore or missing my mother or father. She pushed me in a wheelchair and I pretended it was the engine on a train. We made up all kinds of other silly games, but she told me we had to be very quiet so we wouldn't disturb the other patients. I felt so safe with my special nurse.

The next day, my parents returned and I told them that I had such fun with my nurse and asked for Mary Ann to come back in to see me. No one know who she was. When I described her, I was told that there was no such person on the staff, and that no one by the name of Mary Ann had been working the night before. In fact, none of the staff from the previous night admitted to playing with me to calm my fears.

I am pretty certain that my guardian angel took on the form of a human nurse so that I wouldn't be afraid. She has always been there with me since, even though she hasn't become visible again that I know of."

Cathy T., Oregon, Licensed Physical Therapy Assistant

An allergic reaction to anesthesia almost claims a toddler's life.

Cathy's youngest son was almost two years old when she rushed him to the hospital because she had found a lump in his groin while changing diapers. It was unusual that she had reliable transportation, because she happened to have a Datsun station wagon overnight on a trial basis from a dealer where she had gone to trade in her old pickup truck. Her truck didn't work most of the time, and even if she warmed it up for a half hour, it would die and not start again. If she hadn't had the station wagon, she likely wouldn't have been able to get her son to the hospital.

"James was taken into surgery immediately, and as I waited in the lobby area, a friend suddenly appeared to sit with me. I was really surprised to see her since I didn't know her that well, but she said that she had a strong feeling I needed someone with me and that we needed to pray urgently. In fact, she became extremely distraught as we did so. My friend was praying with quite a bit of intensity that the doctors would know what to do and that what was wrong could be taken care of; she seemed to believe that there was some kind of emergency or problem. This, of course, freaked me out.

After my friend left, I saw a crib being wheeled into Intensive Care and just knew it was my son. The doctors came to see me then and asked, "Does anybody in your family have allergic reactions to anesthesia?" I told them that my brother had had a bad reaction to dental surgery one time, and his muscles were sore for weeks afterward. The doctors became upset at that and said, "You should have told us." Apparently, when they put the anesthesia tube down James's throat, he went rigid with what is known as a massive chemical reaction. A patient will die when this happens about 80% of the time. Because his vital signs remained stable, except for a fever of 103, they continued the surgery and slowly things turned around.

I was convinced that my friend was being used divinely, and that our prayers helped the surgery progress successfully. Although he could have very easily died, James recovered and is now 13 years old. He has regained most of his strength, but still today has some residual weakness in his ankles and legs. I spent a long time being very angry about this, and could have sued the hospital, but I finally let it go. Even though his life has been affected because he can't run and do sports like other kids, we are just lucky to have him alive. He was really being taken care of in a dangerous moment."

"Mary M.", Arizona, Patient Care Coordinator

A magazine offers unexpected guidance in a child's serious medical crisis.

Mary notes that while she was pregnant, she always read a specific parenting magazine at all her appointments at the doctor's office. It was the only place she ever saw that particular magazine. So how did that specific magazine impact her life?

"At age 4, my son caught a nasty stomach flu, but eventually got over it. Two weeks later, it hit him again and then occurred periodically for a long time. His doctor said it was somewhat unusual but not impossible to see that happen.

Right about that time, I received a copy in the mail of the same parenting magazine I had been reading at the doctor's office; oddly, it was addressed directly to me; my first and last names were on the label. But I hadn't subscribed to it! I checked with family members, and found that no one had sent it to me. The issue I received contained an article about how to advocate for a child who is hospitalized, which I found very interesting and enlightening. It would later prove to be a lifesaver!

My son started losing weight, which is significant in a small body that weighs only around 40 pounds. The doctor performed an endoscopy and discovered a congenital birth defect called intestinal malrotation. This occurs before birth when the intestines don't form or rotate into their correct positions in the abdomen during fetal development. It can create a life-threatening complication where the intestine twists, cutting off the blood supply and causing an obstruction. My son was rushed to the hospital and into surgery. He is in medical books today as an early example of this condition. The defect used to be discovered only after a child died, and the problem was found in an autopsy. Now they can operate to surgically repair this and help a child grow and lead a relatively normal life. This happened to my son. He improved and was normal after that, although poor absorption of nutrients has always been an ongoing challenge.

While my son was hospitalized, I discovered that the article in the "unsolicited" magazine was tremendously helpful in showing me how to be the advocate for his care. I was empowered in an amazing way to ask the right questions, to document every single person, medication, and procedure that was involved, and to speak up whenever something was needed for appropriate care. I would NEVER have done all those things without the guidance in that article that had been so mysteriously received.

One dramatic example of that advocacy was when a nurse came to inject pain medication in an IV line. I stopped her saying, "Wait, don't do that, he just received that dose a short time ago." The nurse pushed back telling me that it wasn't documented on the chart, so she planned to do it anyway. I refused to allow it, and when she investigated, she discovered the medication had indeed been provided, but missed the charting. She apologized and said she was grateful that I had been monitoring the medication, so my son hadn't been given an excessive amount.

My son is still with us and I am blessed because of that. However, the magazine that had provided such vital and timely information for me never appeared again."

Lori G., Arizona, Artist

A voice warns Lori away from a potential hostage situation.

"When I was 17 years old, I was shopping at a stationery store before heading onward to the Woolworth's store which required turning to the right. Just before I reached the exit door at the stationery store, I heard what sounded like a car backfiring out on the street. As I got to the door, I had this extremely strong feeling inside and literally heard a voice that said to me, "Do **not** go to the right–go left and go home immediately!"

I turned to the left and began hurrying down the sidewalk with my heart beating fast and a strange sense of agitation. Before I got very far, my boyfriend pulled up next to the curb, leaned over to open the car door. and shouted, "Hurry up and get in."

He explained to me that a robbery had occurred at the gun shop next to the stationery store, someone had been shot, and some hostages had been taken. If I had walked to the right as I had planned, I could have stumbled into this dangerous situation. I'm certain my angels were warning me away from it."

Naomi J., New Mexico, Habitat Conservation and Endangered Species Work

A special son changes dramatically.

The story below is about a very special young man who has lived with the angels for years, and this is his mother's version of her son's "handicap." In Naomi's words (the mother): "I should be so lucky to have this handicap!"

"I have three sons. The youngest, Glenn, is mentally disabled; but is what is called "educable mentally retarded." The first four years of his life I was in an absolute panic all the time...constantly looking for answers, worrying that I would do something wrong that would handicap him further, and constantly overprotecting him from life.

Two days before his fourth birthday was the time I have since come to refer to as "Glenn's day with the angels." He awoke that morning with bright, sparkling eyes; and there was a sense of quietness and peace around him. He smiled almost constantly that day. His usual tantrums, sullenness, and actions of frustration were just non-existent!

I know this wasn't my imagination because my five-year-old son said to me during the afternoon, "Glennie's different today. Ain't he special?"

I found Glenn's new attitude to be contagious. By the time I put him to bed that night, I was completely at peace. I felt more relaxed and less concerned that I would somehow do something wrong in raising him. I seemed to have an intuitive new knowledge...that I could love and encourage him with all my strength, but I would never in my life worry about him again. I was convinced that Glenn has his own special "keepers."

Glenn is 34 years old today, and he is still "mentally challenged," but he has worked for the same company for 11 years and even drives on his own. Although one of his brothers helps him with his finances, in all other ways he is very independent. His "angels" have never left him, and have given him the most beautiful outlook on life. He may be the luckiest one of us all."

Kelley B., California, Human Resources

An obstacle is removed and Kelley is able to avoid a stopped vehicle just in time.

"When I was 16 years old, I was living in El Cajon with my mother and had something strange happen to me as a new driver. I was driving a Corvette on a street that is very poorly lighted, fairly wide with many trees and very expensive homes. Somebody made a turn right in front of me and stopped in the driving lane. I was trapped because there was a car behind me and one to my left side also, effectively boxing me in.

I slammed on my brakes and realized I didn't know what to do. Suddenly my car radio began flipping from one station to the next in a "scanning mode" and everything in my car flew all over the place. The car to my left side disappeared and I moved over immediately to go around the stopped vehicle.

It seemed very strange to me that the car traveling beside me would just all of a sudden not be there, and so I checked in the daylight the next day, and there was no place for a vehicle to turn off where this happened. The curbs were all solid with no side streets or driveways right there. I have no idea how I escaped rear-ending the stalled vehicle, but I was grateful for the help I received."

Reflect and Act

Reflect:

- Understand that the children are protected because God loves their innocence, their vulnerability, and their trust that the world around them is good.
- If God protects children and sends angels to watch over them, what responsibility does that give you in demonstrating that same care for young people with your own actions?

Act:

- To ensure that you are an instrument of protection for God's children, you could protect their physical safety and emotional well-being, be a safe presence

when around them, and love them in practical ways every day.
- To help make the world better for children, discover you could do to advocate for their needs, or speak up when you see situations that present danger for children, such as bullying, unsafe living conditions, or neglect.
- Teach your children how to pray and specifically ask that God send his angels to watch over them.

5

GOD'S LITTLE WHISPERS: THE INNER VOICE

In a world filled with noise and confusion, people are bombarded daily with thousands of stimuli, so much in fact that some of it must be blocked or not given attention or we would suffer from overload. That is the buzzword of the information age... "data overload." We have all felt that sense of being overwhelmed and unable to cope with the sheer volume of information that our minds are expected to process, sort, and use every day.

In the midst of that kind of confusion, how can we be expected to hear a message that is so fleeting, so frail, so gentle that it is like a breath. We are expected to pick out a wisp of a message from a mountain of data so crushing that it could be lost in an instant. And yet, that very message is our lifeline to our Creator, God's voice in our lives, reminding us that all that other "stuff" is meaningless compared to what He has to say. A prayerful spirit helps us to tune back into the only information source that really matters. God speaks to each person in different ways, but we have to learn how to listen. Physical ears don't matter here; it is a spiritual state, calm and attentive. It is a tuning out of all the other stimuli so that God's whisper can come in.

God uses angelic messengers in a variety of ways with humans, and a common occurrence is information that people interpret as the voice of a guardian angel or a feeling or thought so intense that it cannot be ignored. There are many other examples of a kind of "leading" where circumstances happen one after the other in a way that they cannot be interpreted as random, but appear to be part of a plan. We may hear a voice, get a strong feeling, have a sudden thought, or received a mental picture or image. None of those should be ignored. God's plan is always on the drawing board–it is our job to look at the blueprints.

~

VOICES THAT GUIDE OR HELP

Robin S., Wisconsin, Accounting

An inner voice "tells" a father where his toddler son will fall into his arms.

"When my husband was just four years old, his family was building a new house. For part of the time, there was no staircase in place yet from the first floor to the basement, and about a 12-ft. drop existed. A ladder stood in the gaping hole for access, and on the lower level his father had set up a workbench with a light on it several feet away from the opening. Other than that light, the lower level was in darkness.

My husband's dad had gone down the ladder and had told his son to stay away from the stairway hole which looked down into the blackness. As his dad stood by the workbench, an inner voice told him to go immediately to the place below the stair opening and to hold out his hands. There was an urgency about this message that could not be denied, and the man reacted immediately by doing it.

The moment he got there with his arms outstretched, his son fell directly into his waiting arms and his dad just looked down in astonishment. If the baby had fallen to the concrete, he would have probably been seriously injured. My father-in-law does not feel that the voice in his head was some kind of random thing, but a very important message meant to protect his son. They believe that my husband's life was saved and that it happened for a reason."

Linda D., New York, Motivational Speaker

Linda receives a message...just before time stops!

Linda recalls two experiences where she felt a heavenly influence affecting her life. One time was particularly "striking" when she miraculously avoided a dangerous encounter with a huge clock.

Years ago, Linda worked at the New York airport and went through a particular bus terminal at least three times each week. She always rode the escalator. On one fateful day, Linda headed toward the escalator as usual but suddenly heard an inner voice saying urgently, "Take the stairs!" She made an abrupt right turn and went up the stairs instead.

Suddenly, a huge clock that was a movie prop fell onto the escalator with a resounding crash, exactly at the place Linda would have been standing had she ridden it. Linda had no idea that the clock had been hung there as a movie prop, in fact was not even aware that the station was being used as a film location. She had never before that day walked up the stairs rather than riding the escalator. Linda has always believed that a special warning from her guardian angel changed her direction.

Another encounter involved Linda's son.

"I was in a hotel room while attending a convention for a professional association, and my family was there with me. I had been sleeping soundly when I was suddenly awakened by my fretful son. I picked him up and walked back and forth in such a repetitive way that I almost became a sleepwalker. It was a trance-like state. Exhausted, I finally went to sit with him on the edge of the bed.

I was startled when I was restrained by what felt like a hand holding tightly to my nightgown preventing me from sitting down. I realized immediately after that I was in the wrong place and there was empty space where I was planning to sit. The protective hand of God or His angel kept me safe so that I didn't crash to the floor with the weight of the child in my arms. Both of us could have been hurt, but weren't."

Linda shared another sweet and even comforting dream she had a long time ago.

"My beloved grandma died in the mid-70s. She was a woman with a very adventurous, even pioneering spirit, someone who loved people and had a tremendous zest for life. She was very special to so many individuals. Almost everyone commented at her funeral about how it was too bad she missed it since she would have thought it was a great party and would have enjoyed it immensely.

Well, I had a dream shortly after that where the funeral "party" was in full swing, and there was grandma sitting on one elbow, looking out at the gathering and just having a ball. I think she must have been there in spirit, relishing the love of those she had known. It was a soothing and peaceful feeling for me even though I missed her."

God may sometimes let us have these comforting visions so our grief is alleviated by any insights we obtain.

Janette S., Pharmaceutical Industry, Adelaide, Australia

Janette is prompted to move before being an accident causes paralysis.

Janette was traveling to Port Kenny with two other people when she was 16 years old. They were driving early in the morning, before daylight, on a road where it had rained during the night. The surface was slick, composed of loose gravel that wasn't sealed, and a five-foot deep embankment lay along each side of the roadway.

Janette was asleep in the back, lying stretched across the seat, with her head on the side behind the driver. She is convinced even today that an urgent voice pierced her unconscious state, "Janette, sit up!" Obeying it even as she woke up in confusion, a startling thing happened. The vehicle went off the road on the driver's side and tumbled down the embankment, caused by either a momentary drowsy lapse by the driver, or a slippery spot that had spun the car out of control.

Although actual injuries to the passengers were minor, the severe damage to the vehicle showed that had Janette been lying in her original position, if she had survived, she might have sustained paralyzing injuries, possibly even a crushed neck. Injuries of that nature usually cause someone to become a quadriplegic. Janette is convinced that a messenger of God, probably a guardian angel, saved her from serious harm!

Chuck B., Arizona, Credit Analyst

An inner voice helps avoid a motorcycle and truck collision.

"My friend was riding his motorcycle on a blind hill and had an inner voice urge him to turn to the right and get off the road immediately. He did so, and within seconds a truck came around a blind curve in the wrong lane and could have caused a collision. My friend felt he was saved from harm."

"I have a cousin who experienced a special help when she was very young, about 8 or 9 years old. She had to cross a very busy multi-lane street all alone and was frightened because she didn't know how to deal with all the traffic. She was crying and wished for help and almost instantly found herself on the other side. She told us that she didn't know how it happened, because she doesn't remember crossing the lanes."

Deborah B., Birmingham, England, Receptionist

A sudden operation proves that Deborah was right all along.

Deborah tells of a very frightening situation where she almost died because no one would listen to her when she tried to tell them that something was wrong with her. She began to find her stomach protruding and went to several doctors, all of whom refused to take her seriously. "I would tell the doctors that I didn't feel right, that something was definitely wrong with me, that I could feel something moving inside of me and so on, but they all said I had nothing to worry about. I even remember one doctor saying in a very condescending way, "It's normal for a woman to have a larger stomach as she grows older; at your age you must accept the fact that your stomach will be less flat than when you were younger."

I couldn't believe he was saying that to me--I was 28 years old! What really hurt was that my family didn't believe me either; they would all tell me that everything was in my head and all but called me a hypochondriac. This continued for months until one day things took a rapid turn for the worse. I ate something that caused me to have an incredibly violent reaction resulting in respiratory arrest. Almost in a trance-like state, I felt like I was slipping away from reality and life.

Suddenly, I heard a very calm voice saying to me "Don't go to sleep now. I can't hear you breathing...you must breathe. Everything will be alright." I clung desperately to that voice, which I discovered later did not belong to any of my doctors or family members.

My doctors operated and discovered a benign tumor in my stomach weighing more than 14 pounds, which they successfully removed. I have recovered nicely and been very healthy ever since with no further recurrences of this problem. I am relieved that I survived, and think that somehow the soothing voice that I heard must have been an angel encouraging me. At the time, I was also angry with all of the people who refused to pay attention to me, but I have now let that go."

Bill M., Arizona, Computer Operations

A tiny depression in a mountainside saves a man's life.

Bill was driving to a ski area in New Mexico where he worked when a bizarre accident occurred. "I hit a patch of ice and spun my car. Those were the days when people didn't wear seat belts as frequently as they do now, so I did not have one on. While I don't remember a lot about how I ended up sitting on the side of the mountain, indeed I was found pressed up against the rock, and the car was on top of me. My legs were underneath it, and it came right up to my chest. One of the police officers later said that if I had been just ten pounds heavier, the car would have crushed me. I was actually squeezed into a tiny depression in the rocky mountainside that was just about the shape of my body.

During the wild spin, I must have been thrown clear through the convertible top. Officers noted that none of the glass windows were broken, so I had not crashed through them. The convertible was down, but had been broken through, although I did not have a scratch on me.

A very unusual thing that occurred during this incident was that just prior to the accident, I saw very clearly the face of a dear friend from the military who had died about eight months earlier. I am firmly convinced that I was specifically saved from harm although I don't consider myself a particularly religious person."

Karen D., Arizona, Computer Industry

A child is guided in healing.

"I know there are angels in our lives, and I celebrate their messages. The earliest and most powerful message in my life involved an incident of healing when I was just nine years old. My brother and I had developed plantar warts on our feet caused by his exposure to group showers at his school. A well-meaning doctor had convinced my mother that the only possible solution was foot surgery to cut out the warts. He terrified all of us with vivid descriptions of aggressive growths driving deeper into our young and vulnerable feet. My worried but resigned mother had agreed to an appointment for surgery at the beginning of our Christmas vacations so that we would have plenty of time to recover. I saw it as a sure-fire way to wreck a perfectly good holiday.

Disbelieving that my supportive mother would buy into such a barbaric solution, I sat stiffly in the back of the vehicle as we drove away from the doctor's office. As I stared absently out the window, I heard a loud, resonant voice behind me say, "You can heal yourself, you know...you do not have to let this happen to you." The voice was unfamiliar, but not frightening; rather it was comforting, strong, and solid, uttering words that

I somehow knew to be the truth. As strange and crazy as it might have seemed, I believed that it was possible to heal myself.

Night after night, I thought about my feet and willed the warts to go away so I would not have to have my feet cut open. Then I stopped doing even that. The scheduled surgery day arrived and we were taken into the doctor's office, trying not to notice the tray holding knives and other scary-looking things as we passed. The doctor poked and prodded at our feet, finally acknowledging in a somewhat bewildered way that there was no evidence of warts on our feet. He then released both of us for a wonderful Christmas break.

I am now convinced that the "wart experience" was my first encounter with my angel who has since entered my life on a few other occasions, always setting in motion the next life lesson for me. The understanding given to me at nine years old has continued to have an impact on what I have done in my life. I now work in the healing arts with my hands and know that flowing through them is a tremendous gift of healing for others as well as myself. So that is why I celebrate the presence of angels in our lives."

Debbie L., Michigan, University of Michigan employee

To her dismay, Debbie's suspicions about losing her baby come true.

"Once when I was carpooling home with a friend from work, we had the weirdest thing happen. We only thought it was weird because we had been talking about our life insurance policies at the time it happened since they had given us copies of our benefits statements that day at work.

So, we're just driving along, and as a lady came passing us on the left, I distinctly heard this voice inside say to me "Lay off the gas." Without even consciously thinking about it, I did take my foot off the gas and we coasted along slower for a minute as the woman's car pulled ahead of us. Suddenly the other driver veered off the edge of the highway and in overcorrecting as she came back onto the road, she spun her car several times right in front of us before she went into a ditch. We literally couldn't believe it.

I know I heard that little voice, and if I hadn't backed away from her, she would most certainly have hit us as she spun across the highway. We checked in the mirror and some other people had stopped to help her so we just drove on, but we really felt like someone had been taking special care of us. We also decided that maybe we shouldn't talk about life insurance in the car."

Debbie also experienced unusual warnings about her babies when she was pregnant and firmly believes that this was God's way of preparing her for one of the most painful things that a mother can go through. She was pregnant with her second child and was told by her doctors that there were some additional risks because of diabetes that had developed since she'd had her first. They did not, however, lead her to believe that the problem was serious.

By the third month Debbie was feeling very strong suspicions that the baby wouldn't live and became convinced that God was trying to tell her that this baby was not to be a part of her family. In trying to share this with her husband, Debbie met with quite strong resistance because he did not want to hear any negative news. But Debbie did not change her inner conviction that God was trying to send her a very important message.

Early in her eighth month, she went into labor and delivered a baby boy who initially did well, but suddenly reversed his condition and died after 36 hours. "You know, I was so convinced that I was getting a message about the baby that I never even bought any baby clothes, which was really unusual for me. Friends wanted to give me showers, and I put them off, saying that I wanted to wait until after I took the baby home. But in my heart of hearts, I knew for sure that I wouldn't be taking that baby home. It was just easier to say that to them than to constantly be sharing the inner message that kept coming to me. I know God was sending me a special communication to let me prepare myself so I could handle the loss."

Debbie ultimately had a third baby successfully, and interestingly enough, never did have any qualms or premonitions about that child and felt quite peaceful and confident the entire pregnancy. On the day she found out that she was carrying her fourth child, to her dismay the inner messages returned.

As she was driving toward her mother's house to share the good news, a chilling realization swept over her: this baby is not going to survive. Debbie almost wept in the car as the familiar voice told her that same inner warning. "No, no," she wanted to scream, "Please don't tell me that again. I can't do this again." The calm voice comforted her, but gave her no hope that the reality would change. Debbie knew that she would miscarry. She reached her mother's house about 20 minutes later and discovered that she had started to bleed. In despair, she knew the inner voice was right...again.

She did, indeed, miscarry her fourth baby the following day. "I was never afraid of that inner voice because I knew that it had my best interests at heart, to help me prepare for a difficult time. I know God and his angels were beside me every step of the way bearing me up when that pain only a mother can feel became too great."

Cathy K., California, Artist and Speaker

Cathy is taught how to heal her badly injured leg.

"I have had numerous times in my life where I have felt a guiding and protective influence, or a kind of helping presence. One special encounter occurred when I was in a head-on collision, and was in the hospital with serious leg injuries. I was depressed and feeling apathetic one day when a man came in, walked over to me, and said very clearly, "How do you see your leg?" I thought, "What a weird question..." I responded, "Well, it's broken in four places...it's in pretty bad shape." He replied in a distinct voice, "It's most important that you see your leg as already healed."

With that, the visitor left, and Cathy never saw this person again. He apparently was not a member of the hospital staff because no one recognized the description she gave, and

Cathy had trouble believing that a stranger would walk in off the street and make this kind of statement. She could only deduce that it was a special messenger who was supposed to help her learn how to overcome the barriers to her own healing.

She ultimately followed the visitor's advice, and created healing images that eventually accomplished their purpose...making her whole and well again.

A more dramatic example of being helped occurred the time Cathy was driving behind a truck that was towing a trailer. A small inner voice told her to get out of that lane, which she did, just before the truck swerved unexpectedly causing the trailer to fishtail. If Cathy had remained in the lane, she very likely would have been struck by the uncontrolled trailer or involved in an accident caused by some other vehicle affected by it. She was thankful for the inner guidance that prevented a dangerous situation.

Cathy also experienced an extremely unusual "leading" toward a new career when she was approached by one of her students who had attended a seminar conducted by an international training company. The student said, "You should be doing this..." Within a matter of days, an agent called with the identical recommendation, even naming the same training company. Almost immediately, Cathy's sister called with the news that she was getting married, and Cathy planned to attend the wedding which would be held in the same city as the headquarters of the company that everyone had been recommending to her. Since this was in another state, it seemed an unusual set of coincidences. When Cathy attended the wedding, she set up appointments with key people at the training company and was hired to present training programs for very widespread audiences.

She had seen herself doing this kind of work for at least a year prior to the time she started, but hadn't known exactly how it would happen. She has continued along this same path for this same company for ten years now and has found it to be extremely rewarding and fulfilling. There have been many growing and learning experiences for both her and her seminar audiences.

Penny B., Wisconsin, Retail

What is the voice that calls Penny's brother back to his mother's hospital room?

Penny's fifty-three-year-old mother was dying of emphysema after a valiant two-year struggle. The family had gathered and held a vigil all throughout the final critical period of about twenty-four hours. "My brother finally decided in the early evening that he would go home for just a couple of hours and so he left the room.

He told us later that in the parking ramp just as he was unlocking his car, he distinctly heard my mother's voice calling very loudly for him to come back. My brother was so startled and unnerved by this that he immediately returned. He found all the rest of us gathered around Mother's bed saying the Lord's prayer, and what was most astonishing was that she was praying with us in a loud, firm voice. For so long, she had been unable to speak or even breathe well because of the advanced stage of the disease.

As soon as we finished, they turned off the monitor and Mother was gone. We always felt that she wanted to make sure that her son was with her and the rest of us at that last moment, but no one really had an explanation for what he had heard."

John R., Arizona, Retired Communications Analyst

A commanding voice saves a driver from disaster.

"Years ago, I worked a second job driving a taxi several nights each week. I was on my way home one evening driving my own vehicle when I became extremely drowsy while still at least five miles from my destination. I am positive that I fell asleep at the wheel of the car.

Suddenly, a male voice said clearly and authoritatively, "Pull over right here, driver." Accustomed to such instructions, I immediately stopped near a small fruit stand close to a major crossroad in a rural area. I sat waiting for my passenger to get out. When nothing broke the silence, I turned to see if the rider needed assistance. No one was there! Recognizing that I was in my own car and of course, couldn't have a passenger, I realized that my guardian angel must have been with me at that moment of critical need. I had no trouble staying awake the rest of the way home!

FEELINGS THAT GUIDE AND ASSIST

Linda F., California, School District

Linda's sensitivity to her brother's dilemma has her praying for his safety at the moment that he is in the gravest danger.

"One of my brothers, who is a truck driver, had a most extraordinary experience. He was driving in a mountainous area between Los Angeles and Bakersfield, an area called the "Grapevine", and he lost the brakes on his truck. It was out of control, and since he was unable to stop it, the vehicle was continually gaining speed. At one point, he was going over 90 mph downhill on a curving road. To avoid some stopped cars in one place, he even had to swerve over and drive on the opposite side of the highway.

At a weigh station, a parked police officer saw my brother weaving in and out, speeding of course, and pulled in with him. When the officer realized the truck was without brakes, he tried to run interference the rest of the way down the mountain. This went on for 18 miles in a downhill run that lasted over 30 minutes. They finally got to a flat place at the bottom of the mountain and he got the truck stopped.

When my brother climbed down after this was all over, his knees nearly buckled under him. He said, "I was so weak I could barely stand. Somebody was sure helping me get off that mountain." The police officer congratulated him in amazement, "Boy, I don't know how you did that. It was really something!"

What amazes me is that at the time this was going on, I had a flash of fear that something was happening and that my brother was in grave danger. I couldn't have had any idea what it was, but I began to earnestly pray for him and asked God to send his angels to watch over my brother and to let everything be all right. I felt more peaceful after I prayed and not so fearful, but you can imagine how horrified I was to hear of the seriousness of this situation.

My brother had gotten on his radio to someone he knew and was telling this other driver to call his family and tell them that he loved them. He was really convinced that he was going to die. My brother has sometimes been amused at my dedication to spiritual things, but I think that after this he will view things quite differently. He knows God and the angels were right in his cab during that wild ride!

One other time a different brother, Danny, was in an accident, and I was notified that I should go to the hospital immediately. I asked if this had happened in a car." "No", they replied, "He was on a motorcycle." This scared me to death and I started praying for the Lord to be with him. I was just driving along, praying as I went.

A sudden thought came to me to turn on the radio, and the lyrics of the song that was playing were: "...He is there, He is there, He has risen from the dead and He is there..." What popped into my head is that it was a sign to me that God was with my brother and the doctors, and I shouldn't worry.

My brother remained in a coma for almost a week. I maintained an almost constant prayer vigil for him. I was in the chapel one day when I noticed two plants on the altar. One was beautiful, lush and green; and the other was withered and dry. I uttered a prayer that God would bring that plant back to life as He would also bring my Danny back.

The next day when I went into the chapel, the staff was replacing the dead plant with a fresh new one. I asked, "What are you telling me, God? Is this a fresh plant like a new Danny?" Shortly after that, Danny came out of the coma, although he was left with a serious brain injury. He really is a new Danny that we have had to get used to, but we are just grateful that he is alive. After almost a year, he has returned to his job, and has undergone extensive therapy, but otherwise is recovering better than expected."

Dixie A., Wyoming, Electrical Contracting

A sudden understanding: My mother will not be with me much longer.

During a lengthy lunch one time, Dixie and her mother were casually reminiscing about important events in their lives. Her mother especially was caught up in a dreamy reverie that seemed like much more than idle chatter over dessert. Although the meal and the memories were pleasant, Dixie couldn't shake the feeling that a more serious event was taking place, and her mother was reviewing a life that was nearing its end.

"I left that lunch with the most intense conviction that my mother was going to die. When I went home, I said to my partner "If we're going to move as planned, we're going to have to do it soon because my mom isn't going to last much longer." We did move in August, and in November Mom was diagnosed with cancer.

They didn't expect her to last long, but with a particularly tenacious spirit, she made it through into the next year. It was certainly not an easy year, but we were all able to prepare for her to go. How did I know so far in advance what would happen? That comforting little voice inside is there to help us whenever our life events seem like more than a human can bear, and somehow it enables us to get through it."

Harriet A., Michigan, University employee

A mother's worst nightmare becomes reality.

Harriet still carries sad memories of an incident in her family. "My husband and I were returning with our two children from a visit to his father's house when I received a very strange message in the car. It was really just an intense feeling, almost like a voice inside my head, but the words were clear: the worst thing that would happen to us in our entire lives would happen the next week.

I was afraid to even share this thought with my husband, so I kept it to myself. But it did happen. The next week, our 21-month-old son who was perfectly healthy up until that time died from Sudden Infant Death Syndrome (SIDS), which gives you no warning of any kind. I don't know how I could have predicted or anticipated this myself since it would have been the farthest thing from my mind, so it must have been a warning from someplace else.

Ultimately, I feel that sensation I had gave me a kind of preparation, although nothing really prepares you for the suddenness of losing a child."

Tim K., California, Plumber

A mother "sees" her family exactly as it turns out.

"A really odd thing happened in our family. My wife made a comment to me one time, before we had any children by the way, that she "saw herself surrounded by boys." We later had two sons. Then we had a daughter, who was our beautiful little angel, but tragically lost her to meningitis at only three months old. It was a terrible shock to us to lose that wonderful and special child.

We later had another son, so that we ended up with a total of three boys, exactly as my wife had somehow sensed. We did have a picture to remember our daughter by, an impulse photograph taken at a store just a few days before she died. We did not know anything would happen at that time, just spontaneously had the picture taken, and have always treasured it.

Dealing with this loss has taken a tremendous amount of faith on our part, but we do believe that some particular purpose was served by sending this daughter to God so quickly."

THOUGHTS THAT GUIDE OR HELP

Annie L., California, Credit Assistant

A young woman is strengthened during an assault.

"After work one night, I was getting into my car in the parking lot of a shopping center when a horrible incident occurred. I was about 19 years old at the time, and as I reached into the car to grab a towel to wipe the windows, I was pushed roughly inside by a large man with a 12-inch hunting knife who had come up behind me. As I struggled, I prayed frantically, "God, I don't want to die!" My left hand was gashed as I tried to push the knife away.

Suddenly, a thought came strongly into my mind...let him do what he wants, as long as he puts that knife in the back seat. I told him that, and amazingly he did as I asked. After he assaulted me, he told me that he didn't feel so great about it, but that I was the first woman he had seen since he was released from prison. So, I was just in the wrong place at the wrong time, but I believe God was there to bring me safely out of that. I had a friend help me get to the hospital to get my hand stitched, and my boyfriend persuaded me to file a police report, but nothing came of it.

The year after this happened, I became involved with a loving and educational ministry that brought me peace through the greatness of God's Word. I spent several years doing missionary work in various cities around the country sharing with others the goodness of our heavenly Father."

Sara H., Pennsylvania, Nurse

Sara has an important opportunity to talk with a good friend...just in time.

"When I was living overseas in Milan, I began to think persistently about a dear friend in Nebraska. I had no reason to believe anything was wrong; I just couldn't get her off my mind. Florence was 90 years young, an extremely healthy woman who practiced a holistic attitude toward life and health.

Because I couldn't stop thinking about her, I called from overseas and was very concerned that she "didn't sound right..." She told me only that she had hurt her back and was in some pain from that. Still not convinced, I called our minister and inquired about Florence, and discovered that despite her denials, she was extremely ill. Devastated, I contacted her again for a longer talk and was so grateful that I did since she died barely one week later. If I hadn't listened to that 'inner voice' I may have taken Florence at her word that she was fine, and not followed up to have the talk that helped me with closure."

Lynn L., Minnesota, Environmentalist

A husband and wife develop an uncommon communication.

"My husband and I have been married just over a year, but have discovered something very interesting. We find that many times during a day, we anticipate the other one's needs, or finish each other's sentences, or say something the other one has been thinking.

We are both Catholic and our religion is very important to us, so we often pray together. When we do this, we feel like we have an audience...that is the only way to describe it. We believe that our guardian angels are listening in and praying with us. We have even gone so far as to name them.

One specific example of how they work with us was the time I was saying my night prayers, and right in the middle I remembered a meeting my husband had the next day, but had forgotten about. He had planned this for over a month, but had spoken of other things he intended to be doing the next day. I woke him up to remind him of his meeting, and he was very grateful, but I told him to be thankful to God instead since that was where the reminder came from.

We both believe that our guardian angels are working together, and that is why we think and feel things simultaneously. Of course, people would say we are crazy if we ever told them that we think this, so you are the first person we have shared this with."

MENTAL PICTURES OR IMAGES THAT GUIDE AND LEAD

Yolanda (Yolie) C., Arizona, Newspaper Editor

Yolie seemed to receive information about her children, but not in time to help them out of difficult situations.

When her son was about 4 or 5 years old, Yolie was watching television one time when she had a vision of a dresser falling on her son. A few moments later, she heard a cry from another room, and raced in to find the child under a dresser. He had pulled out the bottom drawer, stood upon it, and indeed had tipped the piece of furniture over on himself.

Another time, while visiting a girlfriend, she saw a mental image of her son being hit by a hula hoop near his eyes. A short time later, that is exactly what happened. Her friend's daughter was playing with a hula hoop and accidentally hit her son with it, and gave him a black eye.

In each case, Yolie was receiving guidance, but either did not know how to interpret the messages, or did not act quickly enough. What she has learned is that she needs to react immediately when she receives mental messages. She feels both fortunate to receive these and yet carries a weight of responsibility with them also that can almost become a burden at times."

Patricia A., New York

A mother's vision assures her that she is being a good parent.

"Life was a struggle for my husband and me, although God had blessed us with four healthy children. It was what we had always hoped for. As the children grew, we knew that we couldn't always give them the "extras" that they wanted; however, they did have a loving and sufficient home. Sometimes I compared what they had to what other family members were able to give their children and felt somewhat guilty. Maybe if we hadn't had so many children, we would have been able to give more to them...

While I didn't share these thoughts with others, they occasionally weighed heavily on my heart. One day, when my thoughts were particularly gloomy, a true blessing from God came to me. I had a vision and I heard a voice. What I saw was an endless road, and what I heard was a strong voice telling me, "I have many things planned for your children and I don't want them like the others." It was an extremely strong statement, but somehow soothing to my soul. As the voice communicated its message, I realized that I was repeating in awe, "Praise God, praise God..." It took a moment for me to be aware that the words were tumbling from my lips, since this wasn't an expression I typically went around the house saying to myself.

Although I wasn't told what the plans for my children's lives are, I have never doubted that it is true and that God had guided us to prepare them exactly the way he needed. I never again questioned or discounted the environment we had created or wondered about what we "should have" given to them."

UNUSUAL WAYS THAT PEOPLE ARE LED AND GUIDED

Ellie L., Arizona, Administrative Support Staff

What led Ellie to her destination? An angel or a sign?

"I met a new friend, Lois, while attending Mass at St. Augustine's Cathedral, and we found that we both shared a strong devotion to the Blessed Mother. Lois attended wonderful services at a place called The Novitiate and invited me to join her. So, we did arrange to meet on a Saturday morning at 9 a.m. Lois had given me careful directions, but I was unprepared for the extensive road construction I encountered when I neared the location. The highest dirt piles I had ever seen lined the roadway. I was supposed to be able to see the pink building easily, but that wasn't possible.

I had a terrible time with the construction and I didn't see any building; I just kept going and going until I was way past where I was supposed to be. Finally, I turned around and looked again coming back the other way. Nothing! Frustrated, I decided I just couldn't find The Novitiate and planned to go home and try again another time.

Just at that moment, I spotted a small pink, triangular "A-frame type" sign on top of a dirt pile. It said Novitiate in black letters with an arrow. I followed the sign, turning into an almost invisible dirt driveway, and discovered the building I was seeking right there behind the piles of dirt. What a relief!

Once I got inside and found my friend Lois, I expressed my frustration about being lost. Lois said to me, "I just knew you were lost when you weren't here on time, so I sent my angel to find you and bring you here." I laughed appreciatively and said, "Well, I'm grateful for the angel, but it was really the little sign on top of the hill that got me here." "What sign?" Lois asked quizzically. She had not seen the little A-frame and neither had any of the other attendees. In fact, many of them said that if they hadn't been there before, they wouldn't have been able to find their way.

I knew I had seen the sign so I said to Lois, "C'mon, follow me out and I'll show you exactly where it is." She did that, and as we stopped our cars at the end of the driveway, I stared in confusion at the now empty top of the dirt pile. There was no sign!

Lois was convinced that the angel she had sent was the one who really helped me, and I began to realize that too. It made me understand the power that exists when we send our angels to others, and I have done that myself since."

Jill F., Iowa, Computer Service

A young wife is led to gather crucial evidence at a crash site.

"My husband was killed in a plane crash in 1977, and it was very sad because we had three young children at the time and he was only 32 years old. I don't know what prompted me to go to the scene of the accident, but I felt that I just had to do it, even if it would be very hard emotionally.

I collected some information at the scene and put it into a scrapbook of stuff I was saving which later became critical evidence in a court trial. They were trying to say my husband was at fault, that he had been flying the plane, but he had not been. The evidence that I could produce made all the difference in the world to the lawsuit, and a settlement was reached that otherwise might not have been. I think

maybe God or my husband inspired me to go to the crash site."

Kim N., California, Orthodontics

A mother's urgent request for seat belts becomes critical one minute later.

"I was driving in a car with my three kids one time, and we were doing one of our trips to Grandma's house. These were familiar streets that we had traveled many times before. Suddenly, for some reason that I can't begin to understand, I turned to my kids in the back, and spoke to the oldest, "Nick, do you have your seat belt on?" "Yes, Mom", he said, with a tone that indicated that he thought I worried too much about things.

Barely a minute later, I was struck by another vehicle and we were all seriously shaken up, but no one was hurt because we did have the seat belts on. Was this just a mother's intuition, some kind of sixth sense, or a little help from above? I don't think intuition really explains this kind of incident."

Nancy C., Minnesota, Utility Company

A terrified woman is guided to the hospital with her stricken husband.

"My uncle was having a heart attack and wanted to go by car to the hospital, refusing to call an ambulance. He wanted to go to the hospital where my aunt worked because he knew people there and probably thought the ambulance drivers would take him to the hospital of their choice, not his. Now my aunt doesn't drive, although she did have a permit, but she really is not very comfortable with traffic.

My poor aunt found herself driving through nerve-wracking rush-hour traffic and was of course upset already about her husband struggling beside her. However, she got to the hospital safely, and raced into the emergency room to get help for her husband. She had left the car right outside the ER door, and when she went out to move it, she was literally unable to turn the key to start the car. She couldn't remember how to drive or how to move the vehicle. Her mind was completely blank.

Now, we all know that it was probably just the stress and shock about her husband setting in, but we always felt that *it was somewhat of a miracle that she got to the hospital* at all. It's true that people can do under pressure more than what they are normally capable of, but we would all like to believe that she had just a little help from heaven."

Christina O., Arizona, Administrative Clerk

A newspaper holds the key...

"When my husband was discharged from the military, we stayed in Colorado because he had last been stationed at Lowry. We were struggling financially, and one day at the Collection Agency I worked for I was having a particularly low day. I don't think I could have felt more down or depressed. Sitting at my desk, I put my head in my hands and just thought, "God we are not going to make it. What are we going to do? Please help us."

At that very moment, the air conditioning near me clicked on with such a noise that I look up, startled. As I watched, the draft from the vent blew a newspaper off the end of a table. I walked over to pick it up and noticed that it had fallen open to the want ads. Curious, I checked the front page and realized that it was the New York Times. "Boy, it looks like a lot of jobs are available in New York," I thought idly.

As I returned to my desk, my mind began to drift, and I wondered, hmmm...New York. Why hadn't we returned there when Ray's tour of duty was up? Didn't the government have to send you back to the place where you enlisted from? I mentioned this to Ray, and he said, "Well, yes they are supposed to ship you back to your home town," but there were very specific deadlines, and he was certain that they had passed long ago.

I asked him to check into it anyway, which he did the very next day. Unbelievable! The deadline to apply for returning to the place of enlistment was 160 days from discharge, and for us, that meant our opportunity was due to expire the NEXT DAY! We went ahead and applied, and the government moved us to New York, which was something we could not have ever afforded on our own.

This turned out to be a wonderful move for us. I found work within a week, Ray found a job within about three months, we adopted two beautiful children there, and we finally got on our feet. Suddenly, we weren't struggling so much financially anymore. Clearly, God had guided our move every single step of the way.

Our final change was precipitated by a crisis. We had been in New York for about five years, and began talking about the possibility of moving to Arizona, but had not made any definite plans. In early February, Ray's grandfather in Puerto Rico became very ill, and his family asked us to come and help. When I spoke to my bosses, they were quite unsympathetic, and refused to allow me the time off. I was adamant, however, because my mother-in-law had never asked a thing in the eight years of my marriage. This was important to her, and I told them I needed to go. I ended up quitting that job and heading towards Puerto Rico. Unfortunately, grandfather died as we were traveling, so we arrived for a funeral.

Upon our return, since there was no job holding us, we talked again about moving to Arizona, prayed hard for guidance, and felt that we were being encouraged to go. As before, I found a job immediately, and Ray did too within a couple of months. We did well, and finally had our own home within two years, and are now happily settled. We believe that our different life passages were all part of a design for us and that we simply had to be open to the possibilities and follow the guidance. Everything ultimately worked out in our favor."

Pam A., Missouri, Airline Reservation Representative

A young mother is given the information that offers her enough courage to end a failed marriage.

"I was married very young--at 17--partly out of rebellion to my family, and partly because I thought I had to since my boyfriend wanted it. I had very low self-esteem! Our marriage lasted four years, and produced two children, but became increasingly intolerable because of the abusive behavior my husband had begun to demonstrate.

By the fourth year of our marriage, I started to be suspicious that my husband was having an affair. I was afraid to say anything or ask him about it, however, because I had absolutely no proof and didn't know what he would do. So, I kept quiet out of fear.

One time he didn't come home, so I decided to go out and find him in the middle of the night and confront him. I put my two children in the back of the car and started looking for him. First, I checked several places I thought he might be but decided to go home when I didn't have any luck. It was like looking for a needle in a haystack anyway.

I was getting low on gas, so I decided to stop and fill up on my way back. I came to a "T" intersection where two gas stations were and you could stop no matter which way you turned. Normally, I made a left turn at this corner and would have gone to the station on the left. I started to do so but had this very strong urging inside to turn right and go to that station. I hardly ever went that way and kind of surprised myself by responding to that little voice inside and going right.

I pulled into the gas station and drove around to the pump which caused me to face the back side of the bar next door. There was my husband's truck parked next to the van of the woman I suspected he was seeing! So, I had the proof I needed to confront him about his infidelity. Getting that proof gave me the courage to finally do what I needed to do and end this damaging relationship. I really feel someone was watching out for me that night as has happened so many times in my life. I have often felt protected and taken care of by some force or being greater than me like one of God's angels. It has given me comfort when I needed it. I know I couldn't have escaped from that marriage on my own, and who knows how much more I would have had to put up with? It's nice to know I'm not alone."

Georgia P., Michigan, Dental Office

A job offer comes at exactly the right time.

As a homemaker and mom raising a family, Georgia had not worked outside the home in over 35 years. One day, someone approached her with an unusual request; her dentist called and with no warning asked if she would like to work at the dentist's office.

Now Georgia had not even been looking for a job, and this was rather a strange offer since in her mind, she didn't have any particularly marketable skills. "I'm not sure I can do what you need," Georgia insisted to the doctor. "Do you talk on the phone?" asked the dentist. "Yes," said Georgia. "Do you balance your checkbook?" Again, Georgia said, "Of course." "Well," said the dentist, "that's what I'm looking for, and I think you could do this very well." And even Georgia thought she might be able to take on this new challenge after those encouraging words.

She weighed the offer carefully, and slowly decided that maybe she should try this. However, as soon as she called the dentist and said that she would like to accept the offer, doubts set in, and she decided that maybe it was more than she was ready for after all. She intended to call the doctor and tell her that something had come up and she would not be able to adjust her schedule to take the job.

As she picked up the telephone, a small voice in her head said, "Do not refuse this job. It is important that you do this work." Georgia was puzzled. What kind of encouragement was this? What was this odd little voice? Although she tried to dial, her hand just did not want to complete the connection, and the voice gently insisted that she go to work. Georgia put down the phone slowly and thought, "Well if it's that important, then maybe I should try this after all."

Following the lead of this inner message, she did indeed begin a new career at the dental office. Let Georgia will tell you the rest of this story: "Two weeks after I began working, I was very grateful that I had paid attention to the little voice. The company my husband had worked for during the last 31 years suddenly gave the employees notice that they were going out of business in one month's time. At age 59, it certainly wasn't easy for my husband to obtain another job, and in fact, it was a full year before he was again employed. This was a very tough period for us, but my job at the dentist's office, so abruptly and unexpectedly offered, was the one thing that pulled us through until he was earning money again. Were we helped and influenced by some heavenly intervention? Absolutely."

The guiding messages that we receive are sometimes non-specific in that we are not certain about the nature of the information or what to do with it. If we react, however, by following the lead given, eventually the reason for the guiding will become clear. Sometimes the information is unclear, but the important thing is to pay attention.

Larry J., Arizona, Consultant/Speaker

A career change offer comes out of the blue.

"I was working at a city job and had a background in mental health treatment, and had been told that I could move ahead in this field if I just took a particular class. I did so, and was even to the point of preparing for final exams when I had a major revelation: I didn't think I really even wanted to be in that career field. After thinking about what would be gratifying and meaningful, I felt guided toward working with large groups and made a conscious decision that I would like to explore a career in public speaking. I did not, however, at that moment make any specific changes in my life or job to move toward this.

Exactly one week later, I received a call from a colleague completely out of the blue offering me an opportunity exactly as I had envisioned. I am very happily involved in this career path today and believe that I was specifically led to it."

Betty Jo V., Michigan, Licensed Practical Nurse, Home Health Care

A Sunday vision...only Betty Jo is lucky to see it.

"I was traveling in Northern Arizona and we went into a small Episcopal church for a Sunday service. I happened to be gazing into a beautiful stained-glass window when a ray of sun fell directly through it and I saw the face of Jesus. It was the kind of gentle, loving face that is the traditional view of Jesus. I said to myself, "You're imagining this!" and looked away, then looked back. There it was again! I saw the face a second time, and then when I looked away for the third time, it disappeared. I asked the other people with me if they had seen anything, but they all said no.

I had this feeling of being blessed in a very special way, and it encouraged me to take a more positive approach to my life. I went into nursing training program and became an LPN at the age of 59, a career which I am still practicing today. I did this because I wanted to make a contribution back to society in gratitude for the many blessings I had received."

Dawn C., California, Secretary

Irresistible music in the night leads Dawn out into the dark, and into a whole new life.

Dawn's story is optimistic and positive about how it influenced a major change in her life. "When I was 27, I had probably reached one of the lowest points in my life. I was depressed, unhappy at my job, and painfully shy such that I found it hard to make new friends. I had moved from Connecticut to California and was feeling lonely and sorry for myself.

One night, I woke up suddenly about 1:30 a.m. and heard the most wonderful sound coming in my open window. It was harmony, very sweet and lilting like a madrigal. There was clapping and laughter, but I couldn't imagine a live concert going on at that time of night. I got up and listened for a moment, leaning on the windowsill, and then felt irresistibly drawn to go out and find the music.

I grabbed my car keys and mace, and went out into the night. As I drove around, I began to feel very silly and asked myself what on earth I was doing. The music sounded close and so I kept my window down and tried to turn based on whether it sounded louder or softer. I began to get really discouraged because my more rational mind took over and said to me that it was pure idiocy to be out with windows down on an L.A. summer night.

I turned into a shopping plaza to turn around and go home when there before me was a group of about 20 people in front of a Shakey's Pizza Parlor. They were listening to an all-male barbershop quartet. I drove as close as I could and just sat for a little while enjoying the harmony from my car, and then abruptly got out and went and stood with the crowd.

After a short time, a man standing next to me spoke up and said, "Excuse me, but where are you from? I don't recognize you." He did not say this unkindly, but what I realized as I talked to him was that all these people knew each other and weren't just a crowd of collected strangers. It turned out that they were a cast from a show that was gathered for "afterglow", a celebration that helps them wind down from the high energy of their performance. Technically, I guess I shouldn't have been there.

The man was very nice to me, however, and asked for my phone number and address and said he would send me a flyer about their performances which he was involved in with both his wife and daughter. I went back to the car for a moment to get something to write with, and did not know that while I was gone, he had told the rest of the group about me. As I walked back up to the group, they dedicated a song to me, which I found really touching.

Ultimately, I did attend some of this group's performances, but gained enough courage to start singing with the Sweet Adelines, an international women's barbershop chorus. I had always loved music but didn't have the courage to get out and do anything about it. My most recent accomplishment is that I have formed my own quartet and we are doing very well.

The thing that I want people to know about this situation is that I have always believed in God, but I honestly don't think it was until this happened that I believed in angels or some "other hands" guiding us and playing a role in how our lives turn out. I now am convinced that no matter what happens, it is for a reason. I found that this experience gave me a purpose for my life and although I have always believed in God, I now believe that God truly interacts with humans. I wasn't so sure of that before, because my idea of God was of a more distant Being. The God I know now allows his messengers to really help human beings."

Reflect and Act

Reflect:

- Hearing God's inner voice requires quiet and a space for you to hear a message. What are sources of "noise" in your life right now that might be drowning

out the messages that God is trying to get through to you?
- Have you had moments of clarity, peace, or conviction, even unexpected ones? What did that teach you about how God is trying to reach you directly and personally?

Act:

- What qualities such as openness, humility, or patience can you strengthen to first hear and then trust the gentle whisper within? Decide on specific ways to develop those qualities.
- Determine a way to create a daily rhythm, a space of stillness to hear an inner voice rather than constantly reacting to external stimuli. Can you eliminate some of the distractions and noise that surround you?

6

VISIONS OF ANGELS

Many of the stories in this book are about experiences that people have where they don't actually SEE an angel helping them, but instead have voices they hear, feelings that are intensely powerful, or mental images of things they need to know about. I think it is a rare experience to receive the vision of an angel. In fact, of the hundreds of people that I spoke with over several years researching two books, (this one and *In the Hands of Angels)*, I estimate that about 4% of the people I met believed that they had truly SEEN an angel. That means that 96% of the people had to use faith to believe that what was occurring was help from God or one of His angels.

It is easy for skeptics to scoff at those who have seen angels. Chery A. told me "You wouldn't believe the number of people who have laughed at me when I shared my story. They thought I was making it up. But I don't care, because I know the truth." Some people continue to share their stories of encounters despite the doubt. For others, it was simply easier to not share the experience after being ridiculed, and to simply not talk about it. Even the cynicism of others, however, can't spoil the joy of those who have seen a vision, because forever after they feel special, impervious to the knocks and battering of daily existence. In their hearts, they find a calm center of grounding that tells them "You'll be alright no matter what." There simply seems to be a lessening of fear, and instead a sense of safety and security that cannot be shaken.

Here are several examples where people see a physical manifestation of something they are convinced is an angel. The common thread is a sense of peace, love, and well-being, with no sense of fear. In each case, the person seeing the vision believes that the message is for their welfare and it in some way comforts or helps them.

~

Chery A., Texas, Secretary

A child's vision comforts her throughout her life.

As a child, I remember being terrified by a storm one time. I huddled against the window next to my twin-size bed, hugging my stuffed dog, and wished that it would just stop. Suddenly, I heard a beautiful and comforting voice nearby telling me that everything would be alright. It wasn't my mother's voice but was that of a woman. I froze in my place for a moment and couldn't move; then the voice came again. It was not an ordinary one: this voice was filled with comfort and a very peaceful feeling and I instantly became calm and not frightened. She continued talking to me and I responded. I asked if I could see her and was told to pull back the curtain separating my bed from a storage compartment.

What I saw was the most beautiful thing I had ever beheld in my young life. To this day, I still find it hard to put into mere words the vision in front of me. I saw a very large figure with hair that stirred gently as if from a breeze, but there was no air moving in the room. She wore a cloak that shifted its colors, changing from deep purple to pale violet to blue then bright royal blue. I remember wisps of pink and burgundy and amber flowing through also. The colors flowed and blended like the instruments in a symphony–only God could make colors like that.

The beautifully colored cloak seemed to fill the entire storage area, but I could not see legs, hands, or a face. That did not bother me because I was mainly listening to the wonderful, melodic voice. It was genuinely hypnotic. I remember this angel telling me "I will always be right beside you to protect you, you will not have to ever be afraid of anything." Those comforting words caused me to drift off to sleep, and when I woke up, both the vision and the storm were gone. What stayed with me was the secure feeling that I had a companion.

The words of the angel came back to me when my daughter Stephanie Ann was born. Because she had holes in both lungs, doctors needed to transport her to another medical center in Shreveport. They promised to bring her to my room before taking her away, but I was terrified that the sedative I had been given would put me to sleep and I would miss it. Fighting the urge to drop off to sleep and afraid for my newborn, helpless daughter, I looked toward the window at one point and guess what I saw? There floating in the room was my beautiful angel.

She looked exactly as she had when I was younger. Although she still didn't have a face, there was the feeling of a smile emanating from her. She raised what seemed to be arms toward me and in a flash, I had an understanding–God was watching over my baby, and she would be just fine. All anxiety and nervousness just dropped away from me, replaced by a sense of security that things were taken care of. I relaxed a little, thanked my angel for being there and thanked God for the precious child He had given to me. Soon after, hospital staff brought Stephanie to me, and I had some time with her before she had to leave. Immediately after that, I fell into a deep sleep because I didn't have to worry any more.

When I talked to my mom the next morning, I let her know that I was okay, but Stephie had been taken to another hospital. Mom was crying on the phone and hurried down to visit me and make sure I was alright. I was truly doing fine because of the certainty that my daughter was in God's loving hands. Even today, as a beautiful 7-year-old, she is very blessed.

Every time I share this story with someone, I get a lump in my throat because there are just no words to describe the beauty of this angel and the impact on my life. I don't ask why God allowed her to reveal herself to me or what the purpose was. I just rejoice in the feeling that I am special; and God has blessed me mightily and is taking care of me at every turn of my life. He has given me a wonderful Christian husband, a glorious daughter, and a terrific life. Only God could make everything happen in our life as it has. I don't question; I just accept and am grateful."

Lynn S., Alabama, Data Entry Supervisor

An angel brings comfort to a troubled household.

"When I was in high school, my home was a very uncomfortable place to live. I now know that the term dysfunctional would apply to my family, but when I was young, it just meant putting up with fighting and screaming and fear for the abuse that my mom experienced. I remember even thinking about suicide, although I'm certain I was too young to fully understand what that meant. With a brother in Vietnam and one sister in college, that left my sister and me to carry the burden.

I remember being very afraid in that house, of noises like growls and grunts, and sounds that seemed not human. I wasn't the only one who saw, heard, and felt this; my siblings did too.

My sister and I shared a room in the middle of the house so there was no outside light–only two doorways: one to the hallway, and another to the kitchen. I say this because it is definite that nothing could shine into that area from the outside. One night I awoke to a figure that was glowing and luminescent with a kind of male energy. It seemed incredibly strong with hands that appeared to be folded in front. I couldn't see a face but do remember the figure as very tall. The figure stayed about three feet away and just seemed to stand silently...protective. This wonderful glowing being came every night for about a week or so and the negative energy in the house seemed to dissipate immediately after. I don't remember feeling afraid anymore after that. The noises and sense of a rightening presence went away.

My brother is the one who helped me understand what had happened–he suggested that it may have been a guardian angel trying to protect me and help me get over my fear. When he suggested that, it felt exactly right to me, almost as if "Of course, that's what it was." I have thought that the guardian angel has probably always been somewhere near me ever since. It is truly a nice and comforting feeling."

Rob M., New Jersey, Human Resources Manager

An angel's visit brings a message that trust is needed.

"My family was going through a particularly difficult time because my father-in-law was terminally ill with liver cancer. On a Friday morning in late August, I awoke in the pre-dawn hours to a room that had an unusual "greenish" hue. In the doorway, I saw a glowing woman with long, dark hair that may have had a reddish cast. She appeared quite ethereal since you could see through her, but I wasn't aware of being able to see her face well.

I felt an intensely peaceful feeling come over me as I heard the words "Trust me." I told my wife about this vision when she woke up, and I was convinced that the angel had visited us to tell us that her father would make some kind of dramatic and miraculous recovery. I soon learned that the real reason for this visit was to give me strength to shore me up for the difficulties to come.

Here is what happened next in our lives: that very day, my wife went to work and found out that her job was to be eliminated within the year, my father-in-law died only a month later, on September 26, and just a month after that I had a cancer scare of my own. Three very tough blows in a very short period of time!

The angel knew best, however, when she spoke those words, "Trust me." Despite the hard knocks, we have received some wonderful blessings: my wife found a new and better job and received a raise in the process, we bought a larger house and were able to have my mother-in-law move in with us, and the cancer scare proved unfounded after all. So, a year later we are achieving a new state of "normal." We all miss my father-in-law terribly, which is an ache that is always there, but we know that many blessings have also come into our lives, for which we are grateful."

Kim B., California

A prayer answered...but not the way imagined.

"Some time ago, I was taking college courses while working full-time and finding this to be a difficult thing to manage. I struggled particularly with my Economics class. After taking my final exam in that subject, I was emotionally distraught; I went to my church and sobbed as I prayed for a passing grade. While in church, I began to feel with a certainty that the Lord knew every one of my fears intimately, knew specifically how much it meant to me to pass that course. A small realization grew in me at the same time...if I failed, that would be okay too, it wouldn't be the end of the world.

Shortly after that, I awoke abruptly one night at 2 a.m. to see a man in a long, white robe standing silently in my doorway. He said nothing, did not move, but exuded an intense calm. The feeling of peace was overwhelming and enveloped me like a blanket. I began to reach toward him and felt rather than physically heard his message. "Kim, everything will be fine." He continued to stand there, as I sank gently back onto my bed and closed my eyes. When I opened them, the room was empty. I remember thinking, "I'm sorry to question, Lord, but who is he and why is he here?" With that, I drifted back to sleep. The unusual visitation came to mind several times after that, especially when we found out our course results.

Although I did not pass my Economics class as I had hoped, I know for sure that God heard me, listened to my needs, and ultimately answered me by sending a guardian angel to reassure me. The peaceful feeling I associate with that visit has remained with me ever since."

Ann F., Arizona, Property Management

A dying friend sees invisible men in her hospital room.

Ann and her friend Shary went to visit Mercy in the hospital, a woman who had been a friend and neighbor for over 20 years. Mercy's heart and liver were failing, and she was in very critical condition. As they approached the room, they saw her staring intently at something across the room and thought she was watching television. However, as they entered, they realized that the television was turned off and the room was empty, but luckily Mercy was quite lucid and able to talk.

"As we spoke to her, she kept looking over to the corner and asked, "Who's that man sitting over there?" She asked us three different times. Of course, no one was visible there, so I said to Shary that Mercy must be seeing angels, and asked her, "Do you see anybody else?" "Oh yes!" Mercy replied. "I can see a young boy standing right next to you. Also, an older man sitting in the chair in the corner." I asked her what the man was wearing, and she answered that it was white. Mercy died that night and we have always been convinced that the angels had already arrived to escort her when we came to visit."

Maria K., Arizona, Paralegal

A daughter's vision helps her through a difficult moment.

Maria's husband had a heart attack while attending a family gathering. Originally, he had not planned to participate but changed his mind at the last minute. The blessing about altering his plan was that at the gathering, there were one doctor, five nurses, and a wife who is CPR-certified. At the very moment he needed help, many resources were available. While Maria was inside performing CPR on her husband, a sympathetic family member led her daughter Kayla outside onto the patio, and comforted her as she wept.

Kayla says, "We were sitting on the edge of the patio with the grass behind us. In one split second, I became aware of a vision, someone moving very fast in long, white robes. I didn't see her face, but simply knew that she was an angel. At one point, I saw a "behind" view of us sitting there...like I was seeing us through the angel's eyes.

When the angel appeared, I wasn't thinking anything specific except "What will we do if Dad dies?" The second I was aware of her, I could see the word "PRAY!" in big capital letters in my mind. She was telling me that the only thing I could do right then was pray. As I did so, I was really in awe of what had happened and became more sure as time passed that we really had been visited by an angel that day.

Although my dad was kept alive until the paramedics came and recovered from the initial heart attack, he died about ten weeks later from other complications."

Kayla kept in her heart the memory of the lovely visitor who showed her what to do and how to respond. She has always been grateful for that special moment.

Jane B., Massachusetts, Building Systems

Bill receives a comforting vision and believes he's on the right path.

"My husband Bill and I experienced an incredible thing during a marriage encounter event. We were doing a section of the session where each partner spends 90 minutes alone answering personal questions. Bill was partway through his assignment and stopped for a few minutes because he was feeling some unusually strong emotions.

He stared absently out into the misty day from where he was sitting near a window. Taking shape in the grayish field behind the facility was a man wearing an unusual sweater--brightly colored but translucent like a rainbow. The man was facing away from Bill and must have had his arms folded, because Bill couldn't see them. It didn't seem extraordinary—at that moment! The only thing Bill remembered thinking consciously was, "Kind of strange that he has a sweater on instead of a raincoat; it's wet out there..."

He glanced away for a single second only, and when he looked back toward the stranger, the man had disappeared. The field was empty and the mist was silent. He stared hard but no form appeared anywhere near the spot where the stranger had so majestically and peacefully stood. Bill was disconcerted, realizing he must have seen a vision. He felt first fortunate and then convinced that God was speaking to him, giving him a sign that he was doing the right things in his life at that moment."

Reflect and Act

Reflect:

- How do you personally respond when someone shares a spiritual experience, such as saying they "saw an angel" if you have not had such an experience yourself? Are you open, skeptical, curious, or maybe dismissive? What does that reveal about your own relationship with the unseen?
- Do you believe that you have ever seen some physical manifestation of something that you believed was an angel?
- Have you ever felt a deep sense of peace, safety, or tranquility that you couldn't explain? Could that have been some form of help or reassurance that you didn't recognize at the time? Was there any physical image or vision that accompanied that feeling?

Act:

- If most spiritual guidance comes from impressions, feelings, or inner images rather than visible signs, how can you become more attentive to these very subtle forms of communication in your daily life?
- Sometimes fear—fear of being judged, misunderstood, or seen as wrong—could prevent you from trusting an inner spiritual experience you have, perhaps even an inner vision. Have you felt such a fear? How did you move past it? What will you do next time to trust what you are seeing or hearing and benefit from the blessing this brings?

7

THE AWE OF THE UNEXPLAINABLE

Sometimes things happen to people that are simply unexplainable–they defy logic and analytical examination. These miraculous events should be appreciated and accepted with a sense of awe and gratitude. It doesn't make sense to put them under a microscope. There usually isn't a way to understand exactly HOW these circumstances occurred. WHY they occur is because God has promised us that we have protectors and helpers. In Psalm 91 verse 11, "And God has set His angels over you and charged them to guard you in all your ways. In their hands they will bear you up, lest you dash your foot against a stone."

The promise is clear. In times of danger or threat we will receive assistance to keep us out of harm's way. It isn't because we have done something to deserve this; we receive this purely because of God's merciful love. Therefore, all we have to do is say a simple "Thank you" and acknowledge that we have been granted a wonderful gift.

In the first story, a couple experiences a series of unusual "cautions" that seem to be warning them away from their long-awaited vacation.

Pauline S, Arizona, County Public Works

Pauline and Daniel receive several cautions that their vacation may need to be cut short.

Pauline and her husband Daniel left for a much-anticipated camping and fishing vacation in Colorado. Little did they know that unusual events would ultimately send them hurrying back home. The first day in the Silverton/Durango area was pleasant and boded well for a good vacation. As they approached the rough hiking and 4-wheel drive area near the ghost town at Animas Forks, the first barrier occurred.

They encountered a lone teenager who was injured with a sprained ankle. He had been separated from his group and needed to return to the Outward-Bound campsite, but couldn't walk any farther. The other teens would be returning to the campsite later. Initially, he requested simply that they drop him off so that he could wait for the group. When they arrived at the campsite, Pauline and Daniel made sure he was comfortable and decided to wait briefly to see if someone did return.

While they waited, three people (two men and one woman) emerged from the woods and approached them. The strangers had no backpacks and no vehicle. With a pretext of asking for a can of engine oil, they appeared rather to be closely examining the campsite, the couple, and the teen. Strangers asking for oil? Where was their car, since the campsite was miles from the road? Both Pauline and her husband experienced identical creepy feelings and exchanged covert glances that said, "We better not leave this kid alone with these people around..." The strangers looked suspicious and had weird eyes, as they decided later when they compared notes.

Pauline and Daniel settled in and traded uneasy small talk about fishing spots with the visitors; at one point Daniel casually but pointedly strapped on a belt with a canteen and holstered gun. Shortly after that, the strange threesome disappeared back into the trees. When the Outward-Bound teenagers began trickling in a while later, Pauline and Daniel felt the teen was safe so they could leave.

The second omen appeared as they arrived near the fishing hole that was their next destination. Both felt a wave of apprehension sweep over them as they approached a shallow stream. How odd. While crossing the stream, both heard a distinct, sharp noise as if they had hit something. Concerned, they immediately stopped and checked the vehicle carefully but could find nothing wrong with it.

The couple continued driving on the other side of the stream, up a fifteen-to-twenty-degree slope with a drop-off on one side of the eight-foot-wide trail. With no warning, their camper suddenly flipped over. Momentarily panicking, they got out of the truck and stared in bewilderment, the unspoken question in each mind: What do we do now?

At that very moment, three young blond men with blue eyes came walking toward them. Each was dressed in a yellow rain slicker. One of the trio spoke, "You look like you could use a little help here."

Pauline continues the story. "I don't know how else to put this, because it will sound impossible, but what we experienced was that the next memory we each had of this was of being back in our vehicle with the trailer safely righted, and we were going in the opposite direction, back the way we had come. I don't have any way to explain how or why we were returning, or where the young men had gone. Daniel and I didn't know HOW, we only knew that it HAD HAPPENED.

Deeply shaken, we decided to stop and rest for the night and take the trailer into Silverton the next day to have a professional shop look at it. While we were struggling to get our pop-top up on the camper without much success, the wind picked up and a wild thunderstorm came over us. We couldn't get into the camper for protection, so we climbed back into our vehicle and waited while fierce wind gusts rocked the truck and lightning crackled around us. We looked at each other and said, "This is the third major barrier we've encountered. Maybe we should just head back home. Having decided to do that, Daniel started driving and to our surprise, not five miles down the road, the storm suddenly abated, and we were back in clear weather. We decided to go ahead with our decision to return home and indeed did that.

Our vacation was O.K.--we just took time to do things we never seemed to be able to work into our normal schedule, but two very weird things did happen after that. One was that we learned immediately after returning home that a neighbor, feeling overpowering fear that we were in danger, had been praying intensely for us while we were gone. The other was that we learned much later that the area we were traveling in had a problem with some satanic cults. We were convinced that God had sent us every signal possible to deter us, and had finally just pulled us out of there."

Pam S., Arizona, Customer Support

An unanticipated delay saves a couple from a major natural disaster.

On May 17, 1980, Pam and her husband packed their car and left their home in Tacoma, WA, for a planned river fishing trip. They were headed for the perfect spot in Washington state near a landmark known to everyone as "the old guard shack." There were no guards, and the word shack is very generous, since the actual structure was simply the remains of a long-since-abandoned hunter's habitat. A strenuous hike into the forest was required to reach the shack located near the river. But it was absolutely their favorite spot, and they were looking forward to getting there.

On the way, they made a stop at a sister's family in Centralia, WA, for a pleasant visit spent eating and playing cards. When they decided to leave, they waved goodbye, headed out to their car parked on the street, and…just sat there.

Pam continues, "Suddenly, we both felt very tired and were overcome with a strong urge to have a short snooze before continuing. We didn't want to bother the family, so we just leaned back in the seats and closed our eyes. I must mention that my avid hunter and fisherman husband was one of those people who never needed an alarm clock to be up early for one of his outings. 3:00 a.m. would come, and he would be wide awake. We had no concern about waking up to get on the road to the river.

The next thing we knew, there was a knocking on the car window and our nephew was there trying to get our attention. It was morning! He was up early for his paper route and surprised to find our car at the curb. He was excitedly pointing upward and wanted his us to look at the strange snow. SNOW?

Horrified, we discovered it wasn't snow, it was ASH. The eruption of Mt. St. Helen's earlier that morning was spewing massive amounts of ash into the air. Our fishing trip was interrupted, and we later learned that the area around the old guard shack had been obliterated. Did an unseen hand hold us back? If we had we arrived there the evening before, we would not have survived."

Julie H., Michigan, Printing Company

A wild ax swing should have severed a young man's hand.

"Recently, my cousin Tammy's boyfriend Rob was helping a friend dig a hole for a flagpole. Rob and "Jerry" hit a root and discovered that it was preventing them from making any more progress and would have to be cut out in order for them to finish their job. What they could see of the root appeared to be about 3-4" in diameter and would require an ax.

"Jerry" agreed to hold the root so it wouldn't bounce while Rob chopped at it with the ax. Rob had made several powerful swings with the full force of his weight behind them when one of the swings suddenly descended right onto the top of his friend's hand as his aim went crooked. Rob expected to hear a horrendous scream of pain, and they looked in horror at the hand thinking it would be severed! The full force of the previous ax blows had been enough to both strongly vibrate Jerry's arm and make deep cuts in the wood, so they were not light impacts.

Jerry pulled his hand out of the hole and stared at it in amazement, his eyes seeing but his mind barely comprehending what he saw. Across the back of his hand was a tiny scratch no deeper than a paper cut...no stitches were required, and it was not even an open wound. He also did not feel any pain at all.

Shaken but determined to finish what they had started, the two friends continued to chop at the buried root. After a considerable struggle, they finally succeeded in getting out a large and very oddly-shaped piece of wood. What they had was a wooden "cross" approximately 18" long with a 10" crosspiece and about 4" diameter. That was definitely not your "average" root!

Jerry kept the wooden cross as a reminder of a very special experience...as he told me later, "I'm not a particularly religious person, but I do believe I was saved from harm in that situation." Everyone who hears this story thinks so too!"

Elena J., Arizona, Municipal employee

Can a sleeping family escape before leaking propane reaches an exposed pilot light?

"One time I woke up terribly drowsy because I had felt someone shaking me, but it was hard to focus since I felt fuzzy and thick-headed. I looked for the person who had been shaking me, but no one was there. I started hitting my husband frantically, just pounding and pounding him, and as we became conscious, together we realized that the propane gas tank was leaking.

We woke our children and all escaped before the propane reached the exposed pilot light at the back of the house and caused an explosion. I believe God or an angel shook me awake because the gas was already thick enough to kill us as we slept, and it is a miracle that we were able to get out. Our entire family could have died from the fumes or from a blast if that had occurred."

The next three stories may be unexplainable, but they clearly teach a lesson to the people involved. When we pay attention to some of the unusual experiences that happen to us, we can learn and grow. Kim learns to trust at a time when she could have been skeptical, Jesse learns to give when he could have been selfish, and Art learns to be proud of his faith when he could have acted ashamed.

Kim F., Arizona, Government Transportation

An unusual gift is received in a time of grief.

Kim encountered one of her husband's friends from high school when he came to her husband's funeral. Although the name seemed familiar, Kim had never met him before. As a nice gesture, he invited Kim to go with approximately 100 other riders on a 3-day cross-country trail ride, and since Kim had always loved horses, she agreed to go. She enjoyed the time immensely but experienced something strange at the end of the ride.

The wife of one of the riders (who was acknowledged to have some extrasensory ability) walked up to greet her and asked, "Did you lose someone recently?" Kim did not know this woman and was somewhat startled by the question. "Yes, why?" she answered. The woman replied, "Because I can see him standing a little way behind you."

Not knowing this woman, Kim didn't feel comfortable responding, "I'm not surprised by that. I've seen him myself." However, she thought that as she stared curiously at the other woman. She indeed had been seeing a shadowy outline of her husband in the months following his death, a faint ethereal figure appearing occasionally in her house...moving here and there, smiling, pausing, moving again. She was positive it was her husband.

The woman who had spoken to her invited Kim to visit their family ranch the following week, an invitation she was happy to accept. While she was there, they showed her a horse that needed a home and asked if she was interested in buying it. Kim was taken aback, "I couldn't" she said, "I've never owned a horse, although I love them dearly, and I couldn't possibly afford it." The rancher's wife said, "Don't worry; the money will be there for you..."

Kim trustingly wrote out a check for $600 and bought the horse. Back home, a stranger came to her door within the next few days and asked to buy the car in her driveway. What a joke! The car didn't run and hadn't done so for several months. Kim tried to explain, "I'm sorry, the car's not working. It's no good." The stranger insisted, "But let me try it; I'm pretty handy." She gave him the keys, and the car started easily on the first attempt, as if it were in perfect shape. "I really need this car" he said. "Will you please sell it to me?" The stranger held out a wad of bills, which turned out to contain exactly $600...the price of her wonderful horse.

Kim accepted the money, and the stranger drove her car away. Days later, the police came to her door. They had found the vehicle abandoned and traced her through the license plates. They had no idea of the whereabouts of the driver and wanted her to take care of it. Kim retrieved the vehicle, which continued to run, and never saw or heard from the stranger again. She began to believe that the $600 was to pay for the horse and was a gift from heaven to comfort her after the loss she had experienced.

Jesse M., Arizona, City Utility Worker

A city worker is given an opportunity...will he take it?

I was working in downtown Phoenix and rode with a friend to my job. He parked his car in a somewhat abandoned area about six blocks away from our building to save money on parking fees. One afternoon around 5:00, we walked toward his car while it was still light out. The area was deserted with a few debris-littered, empty lots interspersed with abandoned warehouse buildings. I became aware that an unkempt man was walking straight toward us from some distance away.

Momentarily, I wondered where he had come from since a chain-link fence bordered the sidewalk he was on. I darted periodic glances from my friend back to the man.

As he approached us in the middle of the street, I noticed two things: that he was quite filthy, and that he had piercing eyes. He asked for $5, and my friend said, "No, sorry buddy" without ever glancing at him. I hesitated but said nothing, looking at the piercing eyes which went right through me. My friend and I were still talking and had taken barely three steps when I thought, "Well I can at least give him the change in my pocket." In that same moment, while I was turning with my hand still in my pocket, I paused in disbelief. There was no one behind us! It had been only <u>seconds</u>, but the man was nowhere to be seen! My friend and I both stopped and stared in bewilderment, then looked at each other wordlessly. There was absolutely no time for the man to disappear between buildings, climb a fence, or even move very far away from us.

Into my mind sprang the verse "... be kind to strangers lest ye be entertaining angels unaware..." Somehow, I knew that the man was possibly not human and the feeling welled in me of missing an opportunity that I had been offered. That feeling was overwhelming and somehow sadly painful.

Without really expecting to find him, my friend and I drove slowly down the street peering between buildings for a glimpse of the stranger. And he was truly a stranger. We tended to see the same street wanderer's day after day, and even gave casual nicknames to those we recognized. This man was not one we had ever seen before, and we never saw him again.

The "bigger picture" lesson for me was about being much more aware of those I encounter. I have worked on that faithfully, and have been more generous to others. I have offered to buy people food when they look hungry and sometimes given money. I do not want to miss any of God's other opportunities for me."

Art S., Arizona, Fire Captain/Paramedic

Art receives a dramatic reminder to be proud of his faith.

"I learned a valuable lesson many years ago in the army. I was a sergeant assigned to drive a staff vehicle carrying several important officers including a full colonel and a visiting General.

I had a leather-bound map book next to me in the middle of the front seat because it was standard procedure to carry it in the vehicle. The cover of the binder was that bumpy black leather that is quite common. Because my faith was an essential part of my life, I was also carrying my Bible with me that day. My Bible had a cover identical to the map book (bumpy leather) with a large Chaplain's cross made of real silver embedded into it with metal prongs.

On the day in question, my Bible was lying with the cross facing upward on top of the map book. As the brass approached the vehicle, I realized suddenly that they might think that it was inappropriate to have a religious item in a government vehicle. Embarrassed, I hastily flipped it over to hide the cross, hoping they would think it was a map book. I know I turned that book over!

My eyes were straight ahead as the Officers got in the back. The General commented loudly, "Well, it's nice to see that the troops still care about religion…" Momentarily puzzled by this remark, my eyes widened with surprise as I looked down at the books next to me. The Bible was back face-up with the gleaming silver cross plainly evident on the top. My breath caught in my throat, and I swallowed hard as I realized what had just happened.

An important lesson was taught to me that day…if I believe strongly in something, I should never be embarrassed to admit it, and I should never be ashamed of my faith! God really stopped me short with that experience."

Angels appear to have to work overtime to deal with all of us and our cars. Many people report circumstances where they are aided or helped in various kinds of accidents. The stories that follow are a few of the many situations where angels seem to be "on board": swerves, rollovers, vehicles careening crazily into the desert, bicycle accidents, and head-on collisions. All of those seemed to require the help of an angel to survive.

Chuck F., Arizona, Civil Engineering Technologist

A wild swerve...a railing...a river...disaster or a rescue?

"I think I had a time when I received some kind of special protection that there doesn't seem to be any explanation for. It happened when I was much younger, just 18 years old and working the midnight shift in an Illinois steel mill. I was driving on the river road and had started to pass a car that then cut me off. I swerved further to the left, and hit the median curb, which propelled me all the way over to the river side on the right. (I actually found the tire tracks the next day that showed what a dramatic swerve it was...) I believe that I even blacked out for a moment, because the next thing I remember, my car had come to rest flat against a railing separating the roadway from the river.

There was about a 20-foot drop to the water at that point, so I was very grateful that the car had not broken through the rail. Most surprising to me was that when I examined my car, there wasn't a scratch on it. I couldn't understand how there could be no damage. At the very least there should have been marks from hitting the railing. Some people might say I was just lucky, but I think there was more to it, and that I had some kind of heavenly protector."

Laura C., Michigan, Ball-bearing Company

A broken axle spins a car wildly out of control into a potentially fatal rollover in the middle of rush-hour traffic.

Laura had a remarkable experience with a potentially fatal rollover accident, and she'll tell you exactly what happened: "Last May, I was on a freeway in a car with four other people, three riding in the back and two in the front. My sister was driving the vehicle, and I was the one in the front seat on the passenger side.

Our axle broke causing us to spin across three lanes of rush-hour traffic. We were in the second lane from the median on a road that had five lanes at that point, including one lane of traffic merging in. Without touching any other car in a crush of traffic, we spun wildly onto the right shoulder hitting a small ditch that caused the car to do two full end-over-end flips, followed by three rollovers to the side, finally stopping right side up about 12 inches from a huge old tree.

The car was totaled, but to our amazement we all pulled ourselves out, and walked away from the flattened vehicle with no injuries whatsoever. The police were astounded to discover no one was hurt when they reached the scene. They had completely expected fatalities (one officer blurted, "We thought we wouldn't find anything but bodies") since a recent similar accident had killed everyone involved.

What was also incredible to us was that no other car was touched or involved even though the freeway was jammed--it was like we were lifted right up over everyone. I have always felt that we experienced a divine intervention because there is no other way to explain what was a miracle."

Trena U., Oregon, Insurance Customer Service

An abrupt swerve to safety prevents an accident.

Trena commutes 60 miles round trip daily on highway 20, a two-lane road with deep ditches on each side. She was going home in the dark during the winter one day when she came upon an accident. "It must have just happened because no police with lights had arrived yet, and the scene was just pitch black. All I know is that suddenly my headlights hit a black Toyota Celica parked straight across the right (southbound) lane, in my path. "Oh Lord! Help me," I prayed quickly.

I saw a driveway to my right in front of a house, and I wanted to avoid the ditch, so I slammed on my brakes, and swerved into that driveway. All the cars behind me did the same thing and followed me into that driveway. The driver of the Celica was apparently walking up to the house for help, because a figure appeared in front of me, and my car slid to a stop about two inches behind him. All the cars behind me managed to stop too, so there were no further accidents. I really don't think I did this on my own."

Robert K., California, Financial Analyst

A terrible crash...and not a scratch!

"I was going to see my cousin one time when I was 15 years old, and on the way, I was in a terrible bike accident. A car anticipated the green light and started through while I was heading through the intersection on a yellow light from the other side. The impact was so severe that my bike landed 40 feet away in a ditch and the vehicle that hit it had 55-foot skid marks. I flew over the handlebars and smashed into the windshield before landing on my head on the ground.

Although my pants were split apart, I got up and walked away without any injuries, in fact without a single scratch. I don't believe that could have happened without some kind of miraculous intervention."

Pauline S., Arizona, Librarian

A teenager is helped during a potentially bad bicycle accident.

Pauline's son Jeff had gone to a mall on his bike one summer day. When he was returning home that night, it was already dark, and as he rode along, he turned his head and began watching a ballgame being played in a park. Unaware of his surroundings, he ran into a parked car at full speed.

The impact was so severe that the bike frame was "totaled" according to a repair person, the frame bent badly enough to be impossible to fix.

Jeff reported later that he distinctly felt pressure on his shoulders. Although he was thrown off the bike, he experienced a "soft landing" and felt as if he were being held and supported. The blessing that Jeff experienced was that he received not a single scratch and was saved from what could have been serious injury."

Roger B., Florida

A couple is saved where many others have perished.

"My wife and I believe in angels. On a February day, we told our dog "We'll be right back" and made a quick trip to the grocery store on a rainy Sunday afternoon. A trip that had been made safely a hundred times turned dangerous and potentially deadly on this day. On the return trip, we were conscientiously buckled up driving south on a two-lane road with a 45-mph speed limit. Suddenly, a car turned north off a side street and an impatient van now behind it pulled around the slower vehicle directly into our path.

Jan's question "What is he doing?' was drowned out by my cry "Watch out!" and the sound of a horrendous crash. The next thing we knew we were being carried off to the hospital in an ambulance, and our car was totaled.

Our injuries were serious enough: Jan had five broken ribs and a frontal lobe brain injury, and I had nerve damage to my right arm that required surgery. Interestingly, although we both had months of aches and pains afterward, neither of us had any cuts on our bodies. We are both convinced that our seatbelts, an airbag, and an "angel" saved us that day. The place where the accident occurred has frequent and critical accidents that usually result in death for those involved.

The accident happened around four in the afternoon. I never arrived home until after 1 a.m. and my wife didn't get back until the next day since she was kept overnight for treatment and observation. We do believe in God, and we both believe an angel was with us that day."

Linda S., Arizona

Linda receives incredible protection during a frightening rollover accident.

Linda experienced something that signaled a new awareness in her life. On New Year's Eve, she was driving in an unfamiliar neighborhood, on her way to interview a potential day-care provider. Her then-husband Roman was riding in the passenger seat. Without warning, a car appeared in front of them as she turned, and an accident was narrowly avoided. Roman was angry, declaring "I could have been killed!" since the impact would have been where he was sitting. Linda smiled and said, "Don't worry, you're with me so you're protected..." Even as she spoke the words, a part of her mind was curious...where had that come from? The awareness was dawning—an unusual kind of protection indeed surrounded her.

The proof came not long after that. Linda was on her way to work at an airline when she had a horrendous roll-over accident. It was a gorgeous winter day when it happened, one of those bright, crisp, sunny days that only Arizona can produce. Her car swerved to the side, veered right, hit the curb, rolled end-over-end UP a hill at a golf course (miraculously not hitting any cars or golfers) and then started rolling end-over-end DOWN the other side.

Several strange things occurred as this was going on. Someone was encouraging her to take deep, slow breaths; helping her to feel calm; and cushioning her head from the jarring, rattling jerks as the vehicle tumbled. When the car shuddered to a halt, she hung upside down, restrained by her seat belt, for what felt like forever. People came rushing over, fearing the worst. "She might be dead...she must be in shock." The words swam around her.

All this time Linda was feeling very calm and peaceful. Paramedics arrived and insisted, "Don't move, we'll get you out." They were having difficulty cutting the seat belt and she suggested helpfully, "Why don't I just crawl out?" "No! No!" they insisted, "<u>We</u> need to get you out." Linda managed to press the seatbelt buckle anyway and abruptly tumbled into a sea of shattered glass. She should have been cut in many places but received not one scratch.

The paramedics forced her to lie down on the stretcher, and were determined to take her to the hospital, telling her all the while of potential ear and eye problems; they had seen these many times before in rollovers. In the meantime, Linda had a slow heart rate and low blood pressure—all surprising to the seasoned medical professionals. Linda felt that they were treating her as if she had gone through some major trauma, but it didn't feel that way to her. Linda knew that some unusual divine protection had been given to her. One of the nurses echoed this when she said, "What happened to you must have been divine intervention; it just doesn't seem possible under normal circumstances." Linda agreed that it certainly wasn't something she had ever experienced before, but she knew that from then on something was different in the way she lived her life.

James B., Arizona, Public Administration

A car careens crazily into the desert, and the driver swears he isn't steering.

"In college, I would work really hard to get extra money for the semester, so I was doing twelve-hour shifts. One time I didn't go to bed because I wasn't tired and so I worked a second twelve-hour shift back-to-back. On the way home, I didn't even realize how exhausted I really was.

I do consciously remember stopping for a traffic light, but I have no memory of the light changing, starting up, turning left, or driving approximately one mile. I was asleep at the wheel when I became aware of a voice and woke up to find myself heading for the canal. I was awakened in time to correct my path and get out of danger. I think there was a protective force outside of me that was trying to help me.

I remember another even more critical incident where one time a friend and I were driving from Phoenix to Los Angeles in a Triumph sports car and had probably reached the California side of the border when a bizarre thing happened. We were going maybe 65 or 70 mph when the left front tire broke away from the vehicle and rolled along beside the car, pacing us. The tire hit a bump and flew over the top of the car (the top was down, and we had to duck!) and careened wildly off into the desert. The car tilted at an angle, of course, with sparks flying everywhere and we had a crazy ride: passed over two dips in the road, crossed a bridge, ran off the road, and came to rest gently beside a palo verde tree in the desert. I said to my friend, "Boy that was some kind of driving!" He said to me, "But I wasn't steering!"

We talked about it afterward and he was convinced that there was another presence in the car with us taking care of the driving. We were definitely protected from harm in a really dangerous situation.

Gwendolyn M., California, Real Estate

Could Gwendolyn's fate have been that of her best friend?

"I know that I have a purpose in life and that I have received special help. When I was only seven years old, I used to collect soda bottles with my neighbor and best friend, and then take them to a corner store to get the refunds. One night we were on our way to the store a little later than usual, and it was getting dark already. My mother said it was too dark for me to leave the yard and wouldn't let me go.

My friend, Diane, went without me and on her way home was kidnapped and killed. This haunted me for years because we were so close and I couldn't believe it had really happened. I started having dreams which went on right up until last year in which I was running and running. It took me awhile to realize that I was still running from the memory of that childhood murder. While I know I cannot change any of the circumstances that happened, I now know that there was a very specific reason that I was spared and that I have a definite purpose in my life which must be fulfilled."

Rick B., Arizona, Public Works

Fears for an unborn child prove unfounded.

"I was living in East San Diego and was an Electronics Technician in the Navy. I was moving my family to Miramar (north of San Diego) and had been working hard all day loading a U-Haul. My wife was almost eight months pregnant at the time and was riding in the cab of the U-Haul as we headed to our new home in Miramar. The truck cab vibrated severely, and she complained of not feeling well.

That night she wasn't feeling any better, and by the next morning she had begun to hemorrhage quite badly. Shaken, we rushed her to the Miramar clinic, where they told us to our dismay that this situation was far too complex for them. We were informed that we must go to the Balboa Center approximately 20 miles away.

We spent over 45 minutes in the car in rush hour traffic with my wife in agony. Once at Balboa, we thought everything would be under control, but it all went from bad to worse. The anesthesiologist said that our plans for natural childbirth were out of the question, and at that point he wasn't sure if either the baby or the mother would survive. We stared at him in shock as he suggested that we spend a few quiet minutes together "just in case..." We could only hold hands tightly and look reassuringly at each other, praying together silently.

As they came to take my beautiful wife away, I walked numbly to the waiting room and then went into the restroom where I could have some privacy. I got down on my knees and prayed feverishly, "Dear God, please don't take her from me. She deserves to live." At some point, I simply turned it all over to God, "Thy will be done," because I knew it wasn't up to me. It was truly in God's hands. As I prayed this intense prayer, a feeling of complete and utter peace washed over me. The depth of this is almost indescribable. I simply was no longer afraid or concerned.

I walked back into the waiting room and sat down. Not long after, my wife's doctor came in and declared that it would be a normal, natural delivery after all, and that things were going to be fine.

We delivered a 5-week premature but healthy son, now 21 years old. God truly does work in mysterious ways..."

Patty Y., Minnesota, Research Equipment Sales

A patch of ice on a normally busy bridge...

"I was driving across a bridge to work, and even though I was going the speed limit, I lost control of my car when I hit a patch of ice. As I overcorrected on the steering, I went first left then right and then hit the edge of the bridge railing. In my mind I prayed, "Please help me stop this!" The rest of this experience happened so fast that it is hard to isolate each individual part, but the best I can remember of each step is: my car spun and went up onto the snow-covered rail on the driver's side...the back end swung toward the bridge...I turned one full circle...the car then stopped dead in the middle of the original lane except going in the opposite direction.

What is most amazing to me is that this bridge is ALWAYS very busy, and as my car was spinning out of control there were no other people on that bridge. I know that if other cars had been present, I would have been involved in an accident. I was very grateful that I could drive away from a potentially serious situation."

Kathy D., Arizona, Administrative Assistant

A mother's grief is helped by a sign...

"My 39-year-old sister died, someone who had been very ill with diabetes from an early age. My mother was devastated over the loss of her daughter, and for months was inconsolable. Even six months afterwards, her grief was still extremely deep. One day she was driving and prayed very hard for a sign from God to let her know that her daughter was alright. As she drove, a beautiful white dove appeared out of nowhere in front of the car. My mother felt considerable comfort that God had sent her the sign she had asked for.

In another situation, a good friend of mine was killed in a horrendous car accident. Her aunt was very distressed about this for a long time so friends had taken her to Las Vegas to brighten her mood.

The aunt was sitting at a machine alone when a man brushed by behind her and touched her shoulder saying, "Everything will be alright." He leaned past her and placed something on the ledge next to machine. Curious, she picked it up and took a closer look. It was a shiny penny with a cutout design of an angel in the center. The aunt turned to say something to the man who had left it there and he was gone. She believed that someone was trying to give her a message, whether a real angel had stepped into her life for one brief second, or God had inspired a human to understand that she, of all the people in that casino, was the one who needed encouragement and uplifting at that moment!"

Mary T., Wisconsin, Homemaker

Mary hears strange footsteps as she waits at her sister's deathbed.

Five years ago, Mary's sister-in-law Agnes (her husband's sister) was dying of a brain tumor at the age of 54. It began several years earlier as a melanoma which had been removed, but had returned as the tumor. Mary happened to be at Agnes's bedside the night she died although they did not realize right then that death was imminent.

That night Agnes was very agitated, plucking at and pushing the bedcovers; looking into the distance she cried, "Please Lord, let me come too" followed by less coherent muttering. After finally quieting her down, another sister who was also present encouraged Mary to go rest and promised to keep vigil.

Mary went into the other room where she had the television on quietly and did some reading. As she sat in her chair a short time later, she was startled by what sounded like distinct footsteps walking in a circle around her chair and then around the room. Not long after that, there was a cracking sound like a house can make on a very cold night when expanding and contracting. Mary was so curious about the unusual sounds that she looked in on the other women, but both appeared to be dozing quietly, so she decided to go to bed too.

In the morning, they discovered that Agnes had been dead for some time, and Mary decided that the unusual sounds heard the previous night may have been Agnes looking around her house before she left it. Although Agnes has been dead for five years, she had been in Mary's thoughts just the week before she related this story to me.

Donna P., Arizona, City Court Customer Service

A gate signals the possibility of a presence in the house.

"I had a very unusual experience after my mother died that has caused me to wonder if she was somehow present in our family home after she passed away. I went to the house the day after her death to pick out some clothes for the funeral, and since I would be only a few moments, I distinctly remember what I did: left the back gate (where I entered) open, left the back door open, and had the light on in the kitchen.

As I hurried out shortly after that, I rushed around the corner and almost ran into the gate which was now closed. Mom had always been such a stickler for all of us closing the gate since it wouldn't do so automatically. I was so startled by this that I stopped in my tracks and stared at it, and then walked slowly back around the corner and looked in the kitchen window where I had left a small light on for security so it would seem more inhabited. My dad was staying at my brother's so he wouldn't be alone, and the house would be empty for a few days.

I stood outside the window for several moments with the strongest feeling that someone was inside the house, fully expecting to see a person walk across in front of me. Had someone crept inside through the open door, closing the gate quietly behind him or her? When I saw nothing, I finally turned and left.

I drove a block away before I realized I had forgotten a particular picture that I needed, so I returned to the house, but didn't pull into the driveway. I still had that very intense feeling that someone was in the house. Quickly, I grabbed what I needed and left the second time, still not seeing anything specific.

A week later, I continued to have the strangest feeling about that whole situation, thinking that maybe my mother's spirit had somehow been in the house. She certainly worried about it enough and had kept asking how everything was while she had been in the hospital before her death. To this day, I can recall the strength of the sensation I had standing outside that window looking in, convinced that the house was not empty...all prompted by that crazy gate that Mom was so particular about!"

June V., Minnesota, County Agency/Part-time Commercial Driver

A voice in the night is June's only hope of staying awake.

Approximately ten years ago, June and her husband were acting as a team doing long-distance driving. June usually took the night shift driving, getting up after midnight to take over the wheel. One time, she was exceptionally tired, having received only a few hours' sleep, and fell victim to "fatigue mirages." Those who drive long-distance had told her that when you are overtired, you see things that aren't there.

In North Dakota, it was very early, well before sunrise and there was no other traffic on the road which would at least have helped to keep her awake. When she thought she saw an alligator cross the road, she knew she was in trouble..."I said inside my mind... Girl, this is North Dakota, and there aren't any alligators in North Dakota!" I knew at that moment that I might be in trouble. Suddenly, I heard a very welcome male voice coming over the CB radio, "Boy, is there anyone out there who can keep me awake?" He was echoing my own thoughts! I wasn't usually much of a radio talker, using it maybe once in a great while to check road conditions or reports of police monitoring.

I didn't see another soul on that stretch of road, so I could not figure out where the voice was coming from, but I began to thankfully talk to this lone road warrior and managed to stay awake until my husband came to relieve me. At one point shortly before that, I thought I had seen a dark black truck pass me, but I wasn't sure--it seemed like one of those fatigue mirages.

My husband did hear me talking happily when he arrived in the cab and was curious about where the truck was. I told him I thought one had passed, but he never did catch up to it, although there was no place to turn off the road. He searched all the rest stops and turnoffs but found nothing. To this day, we're certain that someone or something came into the night to help keep me awake and both of us safe."

Deborah W., Texas, Graphics/Fashion Design Consultant

Deborah's health miraculously changes for the better.

"I was diagnosed with severe rheumatoid arthritis, and my body was in terrible shape. I had intense fatigue, extremely swollen joints, blurred vision, and was unable to walk more than a few feet at a time. This, of course, was creating a negative quality of life. The people in my church were wonderful and prayed for my healing. God told me, "You are healed, but you will have to <u>walk</u> in that healing." Now, because of that, I <u>believed</u> that I was healed and began to concentrate primarily on spiritual thoughts and other positive thinking.

I was guided to a doctor in Tulsa who did all kinds of tests and said that my body was struggling because of nutritional problems. He prescribed various kinds of diets, enzymes, and supplements. Although God had healed me, I think these other physical elements did support what was happening in my body. All my symptoms disappeared; I lost 35 pounds and suffered no anxiety attacks.

God took care of me, and I am going to share that gift with others. I am working on a cookbook to help others understand how to take care of themselves to maintain the health God gives them."

Victoria F., Arizona, Technical Editor

A difficult time leads to important learning.

"Did you ever have an absolutely horrendous period in your life? I had one year in which I was very ill with hepatitis, my marriage disintegrated, I lost my job, had three car accidents, had little things stolen from me such as my wallet and my clothes from a laundry room, and finally had my five-year-old daughter hospitalized with a severe psychosis triggered by taking the drug Ritalin. As if that weren't enough, the insurance company informed us they wouldn't cover her hospital bills (which were nearing six figures) because this was an emotional and not a physical disorder.

While my daughter was in the hospital, she began having strange "dreams." She would say things like "I was in a garden, and I picked a flower for you and an angel was there who loved me and said everything would be alright. Then a star fell out of the sky, and I put it back." As she spoke these things, I thought, that sure sounds a little strange. She also began drawing "dreamy" pictures with the most beautiful, vibrant colors.

She seemed to be an almost ethereal child at that point. Maybe her behaviors can be identified by some psychiatrist as part of a psychosis, but I believe she was somehow being touched by a spiritual experience that I can't begin to explain.

I noticed that at this same time other good things began occurring in our lives: for example, an unexpected check suddenly arrived from the IRS (how often do you hear of that happening?), the accident that had happened in a very bad part of town turned out to be with an insured driver whose insurance company sent a settlement check for $1,500. Odd...that was at the exact time that bills in that amount needed to be paid. That money, in fact, tided us over until I started working again.

The lesson that I learned through all this is that when you think you have gotten to the very edge--there is no edge, just another place to move on to. After all the experiences described above, the major result was that I began to seek a more spiritual existence and to become closer to God. We were so clearly being taken care of by someone that it has led to a deeper faith."

Diana B., Illinois, Senior Home Health Care

Two men...transformed in different ways.

"My brother Earl and my nephew Joe and I all grew up together except for the period we were separated when Joe and Earl had to serve in Vietnam. It was very tough for them when they came back, and I was heartbroken that Earl had gotten involved in drug use and alcoholism. Joe lived a more conventional life, becoming a farmer until he developed cancer, which was a terrible shock to all of us. At one point, they even wanted to amputate his arm, but he absolutely refused, and didn't even want to do the chemo and radiation the doctors wanted.

Because we all believe in the power of prayer and the work of God in our lives, Joe was willing to participate in intense prayer sessions, even including a laying on of hands. The next thing we knew, the cancer had disappeared, and he was free of the illness. Truly a miracle!

While things were getting better for Joe, in the meantime, Earl's life was going steadily downhill. By this time, he had lost his home, his job, his wife and was living in a camper. One time he was praying for a conversion to change his life, and he asked for a sign from God that would show there was some hope. Earl was told by a clear, distinct voice, "I cured Joe, didn't I?" This dumbfounded Earl and created a startling transformation in him because he knew God's power was infinite. Well, Earl completely turned his life around and today he is a minister in Alaska and teaches college. Nothing makes him happier than to speak about how God can transform a person, and his testimony is that much more riveting because of the depths to which he had sunk before his rebirth."

JeriAnn, Illinois, Airline Computer Specialist

Johnny's not-so-imaginary friend is a longtime playmate.

"When my son Johnny was five years old, he would talk constantly about his friend "Joey." Now, none of us could see Joey, but we would find our son alone in his room laughing and playing with someone. We asked him about his friend (acting like we knew Joey was there) and he was very open with us. "Joey lives in heaven with the angels but plays with me if he's lonely. He misses his Mommy and Daddy." We were somewhat surprised to hear him talk about heaven as if it were an everyday thing to play with people from heaven. "How did Joey get to heaven?" we asked. "He was playing with his Daddy's shotgun and he hurt himself, but now he lives in heaven all the time." We decided it was probably wiser to let him keep Joey as his friend than to probe more and try to convince him otherwise, so we simply incorporated Joey into our family. We would put a chair at the table or say hello to Joey if we walked into a room where Johnny was "playing" with him. We would ask him how Joey was doing today. The relationship lasted for two or three years and then Johnny slowly stopped talking about Joey and seemed to move on to other interests."

JeriAnn is an interesting person to talk with, funny and articulate. She told me that she felt from the time she was young and survived a life-threatening bout with whooping cough that she was meant to do something special with her life. I asked her if she had done it yet. She said that she had always thought it was supposed to be something big and dramatic, but that she had only done lots of small things. People are always asking her advice when they are frustrated or confused, and she is very willing to counsel them. One time someone talked to her instead of committing suicide. As we spoke, she realized that maybe her special contribution was to always be there for other people, and that too could be a very significant thing in one's life.

When JeriAnn was just 17 years old, she had a near-death experience that changed her outlook on life and made her a gentler, more compassionate human being. She was given a transfusion of the wrong blood type and had a life-threatening violent reaction to it. Her face swelled into a huge blob, and she actually left her body for a time. The experience she related is very similar to what other people tell about who have gone through the same thing. She was in a bright light, felt warmth, and experienced tremendous peace and joy. JeriAnn also had a sense of a loving spiritual companion while she was in that state. For the rest of her life since that point, she has felt an obligation to live a worthy life.

Beatrice L., California, Accountant

A strange example of newspaper photographs.

Here is an example of a small but odd occurrence that doesn't lend itself to an easy and logical explanation.

Beatrice relates the story about the time her great-grandfather was celebrating his 100th birthday at his home in 1932. He was surrounded by many proud family members who had arranged a special treat...one of them was going to photograph the momentous occasion of four generations in one room at the same time. They wanted to have their grandad and his birthday cake pictured because someone had painstakingly placed 100 candles on his cake.

Beatrice says, "In addition to the picture with the cake, another was taken of my great-grandfather, my grandad, my father, and my oldest sister who was just a baby at the time. They were so proud of those four generations! I need to stress that *no other pictures* were taken at that party by anyone else, and there were no people from a newspaper attending. The film was not developed until long after the party.

However, two different members of our family have newspaper clippings with dates showing that both pictures appeared in the next day's edition of the local paper. I'm certain that in

1932 they did not have the ability to develop film overnight. Our family members have never been able to come up with a good explanation for this strange series of occurrences."

Richard D., Arizona, Fire Inspector

Richard sees a peculiar vision at a hotel in Mexico.

"My wife and I were on vacation in Mexico and stayed in a very old Mexican town called El Fuerte, which is in the tropical area by the coast. This town dates back to the 1600s, and our hotel, which is part of the Copper Canyon Train Tour, also dates back several hundred years. While it has been a hotel for at least a hundred years, before that it was the mansion home of a wealthy citizen in the early 1800s.

I was sleeping in my room, but in that lighter "twilight state" that occurs before a deep sleep. Suddenly, I lifted my head, opened my eyes, and saw the figure of a soldier through a kind of haze. He was dressed in an old-fashioned uniform with a carbine over his shoulder, looking straight ahead smoking a cigar that had real smoke curling off it. The soldier had dark hair and a grayish mustache and wore a khaki-colored uniform.

Oddly enough, I was not afraid but felt safe and protected and laid my head back down. When I realized what I had seen, I woke up with a start and sat up in bed. No one was there. I got up and looked outside, even tried to smell the aroma of the cigar smoke I had seen spiraling upward. Nothing. The next morning at breakfast, I told my wife Irene and the tour director what I had seen. The hotel owner's son overheard me, and explained that <u>many</u> sightings had taken place at this particular hotel. He told me that the figure I described was very accurate and would have really existed more than a hundred years ago, and that makes me feel that for a few moments in time, I was tuned into a completely different realm.

I do want to relate one other very unusual set of circumstances. One time when my wife was at home and I was at work, we both happened to choose lottery numbers without having spoken to each other. When we looked at our tickets that evening, all the numbers (unfortunately, of a non-winning ticket) were identical except for one which was only one digit off. Now that seems amazing to me. Could it have been only a coincidence?"

Reflect and Act

Reflect:

- When have you experienced something unexplainable or protective in your life, and how might you reinterpret that moment through the lens of God's promise of care rather than coincidence?
- How comfortable are you with "mystery"—accepting what you cannot analyze or logically explain? What does your comfort level reveal about your trust in God's mercy and protection?

Act:

- If God's guidance often comes as subtle cautions, nudges, or interruptions, how can you become more attentive to those quiet signals and not brush them aside as random or insignificant?
- What specific steps can help you pause long enough to notice when something inside feels uneasy or warned, and then respect and following that inner prompting rather than overriding it?

8

LOVE THAT LIVES BEYOND DEATH

As humans, one of the hardest things we deal with in our lives is the loss of friends and family members whom we love. Of course, they always remain in our hearts and our memories, and we can be reminded of them through pictures, but the physical presence is what we grieve for. We miss touching them, hugging, or kissing them, and just being able to physically see them in front of us to see their smiles and hear their voices.

Love is the most powerful energy that exists in the universe, springing from God the Creator who is Love. When our families and friends leave the physical plane, they don't stop loving those they leave behind. Because they are no longer composed of physical being, but are then spirit, they cannot touch us as they have in the past, but the energy of pure love is still part of them.

Many people have had experiences where they feel the love energy of family members and friends who have died. Occasionally, they seem able to SEE a loved one in a vision, but more often they feel a loving presence that they recognize. People occasionally reported experiencing a sign of some kind that can be anything from flowers to pictures, while many others are convinced that the deceased loved one aided them in a variety of ways, often lifesaving.

The first story teaches us a valuable lesson about how death is not the end of everything for the families left behind, but sometimes just the beginning.

∼

Margaret K., Louisiana, Assistant Professor

An amazing daughter influences her family after her death.

"The loss of a loved one is always a difficult thing. Despite having lost grandparents as well as dear friends, the most devastating event of my life was losing my beautiful daughter, Brooke, who was killed in an automobile accident on August 1, 1994. She had just graduated the previous May and losing her impacted the community as well as our family. Brooke was a young woman of boundless energy and enthusiasm who had received many honors and awards, was active in her church, and worked several jobs.

Brooke had been elected by her school peers as Miss Natchitoches Central High School, was Homecoming Queen, had won Miss Teen Dixie Gem, and at the time of her death was serving her reign as Miss Merry Christmas for the City of Natchitoches. She had presided over the 1993 Christmas Festival, and represented the city by making presentations at other festivals and functions. Brooke volunteered at the church teaching Christian Doctrine classes and serving as a resource person for the Teens Encounter Christ group. Brooke also worked at the local movie theater. One summer she worked three different jobs, doing four hours in the morning at the city recreation department's summer camp program, four hours in the afternoon at Northwestern State University, and four or five hours a night at the theater. We felt it was too much and asked her to give something up. But she didn't want to give any of it up because she loved every one of these activities so much, and it gave her the opportunity to interact with all different age groups.

Losing someone like this seemed beyond belief. I honestly felt abandoned by God. How could He take away a person who added so much to this world? A very dear friend commented to me on one particularly sad day, "I don't know why God chose Brooke; He must have needed her in heaven for some reason. But remember that where God closes one door, he always opens another one." It was so hard to feel that this was not just some pious platitude; what other doors could there be? One thing I did know was that I needed to be strong for my two sons who had lost their sister. They couldn't afford to lose a mother as well.

Three unusual events after Brooke's death showed us the power of love that can never die and taught us a lesson about how God opens doors.

Event One:

On a Thursday about a month after Brooke died, Jim and I met at the cemetery with a group of young women from the university at their request. They presented us with a plaque making Brooke an honorary member of their sorority. While standing by the grave, one young woman remarked that she often came and talked with Brooke, idly making clover chains as she sat there. She said that in all the times she had done that, she had never found a four-leaf clover. I smiled and said, "Well, I think Brooke should just send us a four-leaf clover, then." We all laughed at that. The following Saturday we were at the grave site again with a dear friend, and we repeated this story. As I looked down at the clover, I saw a baby four-leaf clover at my feet.

Event Two:

Jim and I had been thinking about adoption before Brooke's accident. I became much more focused on this project afterward; Jim was less enthusiastic at that point. Originally, we had prepared all the paperwork for the China program. In November, we also enrolled in the Russia program. The week after Thanksgiving, during a quiet discussion with Jim, he said he didn't think we'd ever get a child. I told him firmly that we had done everything we could on the human side, and it was now in God's hands. I really believed that.

On December 3, what would have been Brooke's twenty-first birthday, Jim and I were at home after visiting the grave in the morning. I was sitting alone in the den with a television soap opera on in the background (strangely enough in the middle of a plot line about a couple going to Russia to adopt a baby) when Jim came in to talk. He wanted to tell me about a dream he had had the night before that was both disturbing and intriguing. This was his dream. *God sent a baby angel to bring him a very simple message: God was giving us the baby we wished for; however, God would not reveal the time or date of delivery. The angel asked Jim if he was interested and he said yes, so they went back to heaven together. He entered a room filled with babies stretching to infinity...every baby that had ever been born. He was supposed to choose a child. He immediately found Brooke, informed the little angel that this was his choice and returned home. The baby angel came to Jim and said "I know what you're trying to do; you're trying to bring Brooke back. You cannot do that. Brooke is home with God, her time on earth has been fulfilled, and her work in heaven is beginning. If you are truly willing to let her go, God will give you the privilege of raising another child." In the dream, Jim agreed to the conditions, selected another child (a girl) and came back home.*

Just as he finished relating this dream, the phone rang. Initially annoyed that someone was calling during lunchtime, he answered it anyway while I continued watching the television program. I could hear bits and pieces of his conversation in the background. "Well, I don't know; my wife has been handling this matter...but all our paperwork is sitting in China...I don't know...we could take a healthy girl under the age of five... wait, let me get Margaret." He walked in, handed me the phone, and said it was the adoption agency.

I spoke with a representative who was offering a child in Russia, who gave me sketchy information about the child's background. When the agency person left the phone briefly to look something up, I turned to Jim: "What should we do?" His response was "Let's do what we must to make her our child." We accepted this child sight unseen and by 4 p.m. had faxed all the legal documents necessary to claim the child. Then the <u>real</u> work began to redo our dossier for Russia and have the INS cable moved from China to Russia. On January 24, 1997, we traveled to Moscow to get our daughter. Strange timing or one of God's doors?

Our translator on the train ride to Borovichi told us that our child, Martha, had refused to go with a previous couple who had tried to adopt her, which made us a little nervous. Imagine our surprise when we later found out why. The first day that we were able to spend any individual time with Martha, we showed her pictures of her new "soon-to-be family" waiting eagerly for her back home. Without any prompting from us, she pointed eagerly to Brooke's picture in the family photo album we had brought and said clearly, "Brooke." Even though she did not speak English she could clearly and correctly say Brooke's name and knew her immediately. We were quite amazed at this, but we knew unequivocally at that moment that God's hand was at work here. We did not need any other kind of "proof." We wouldn't find out until later, however, the extent of Brooke's involvement.

Event three:

About two weeks after coming back from Russia with our just under five-year-old Martha, something odd occurred. Martha was sleeping in Brooke's room which had remained virtually untouched since she died. I intended to put away all of Brooke's things so that it could become Martha's room. I knew this would be hard for me, but it was necessary to accomplish. On that night, Martha fell asleep and began dreaming, at one point talking so loudly that Jim went in to see what was going on. She started speaking in Russian to him but clearly saying Brooke's name over and over.

Jim brought her into our bedroom and asked me to listen to her. Martha started talking Russian, walking in a circle, and waving her arms around. Frustrated, I told her in broken Russian that I couldn't understand. She left for a moment, and then returned from her bedroom with a picture of a guardian angel and pointed to it, repeating "Brooke, Brooke." I told her "Nyet (no)" that it wasn't Brooke. But she kept insisting, saying it louder and louder. Finally, to appease her I said, "Da (yes) that's Brooke" and she seemed content. She smiled happily and calmly went back to bed.

As her English improved, Martha told us that Brooke the "angel" had come to her in Russia and said mama and daddy were coming to get her and she should wait. That is why she had rejected her previous prospective parents because they weren't us. Brooke let her know that we were coming. Also, for months, Martha would have dreams where Brooke "the angel" would take her flying around the world. Around the time that she became totally comfortable with her new life (she no longer said "Please don't send me back") the dreams stopped. Over time, we became convinced that this new family member was a door God had opened for us.

We feel so blessed. We often experience little, odd things that we have lovingly come to refer to as "signs from Brooke." We know that she is still very much a part of our family and a part of Martha's life. We know that a loving God does open new doors where others have been closed and we have been given a tremendous opportunity."

Linda C., Wyoming, Switchboard Operator

A young wife hears her husband's voice as he dies in a rock-climbing accident.

"We've had several really unusual experiences with our family members that just can't be explained by any normal means. Our 21-year-old daughter, Heather, was alone at home one time when she very clearly heard her husband's voice saying from nowhere, "I love you." She thought she had imagined it except that it was so definite.

Just barely an hour later, she was notified that her husband, Jason, had been killed in a rock-climbing accident. It would have happened right around the time that she had heard the invisible voice.

Another strange thing occurred several months after his death when she was resting on the sofa one time in an almost dream-like state. Heather had the distinct feeling that she was laying with her head in her husband's lap, and it was a really comforting, calming feeling as if he were there holding her."

Another odd circumstance in that family was when a 4-year-old relative of Linda's was diagnosed with cancer, although it went into remission for well over a year and a half. One day he was playing with his brothers, sisters, and cousins when he announced out of the blue, "Guess what? Next week I get to be an angel." Needless to say, everyone was a little taken aback at this candid, seemingly off-the-wall statement. But the casual prediction came true, because he suddenly died the following week. This was quite a shock because the cancer had been in remission for such a long time, and no one in the family really expected anything to happen right at that moment.

Linda continues, "This example may seem minor and even a little strange, but it did make an interesting impression on our family. My Mom's nephews had lovingly made her a cute green, beaded stiff-wire Christmas tree. She adored that little tree. She became quite ill just before Christmas and ended up in the hospital. The family noticed that when she went into the hospital, the top of her special little tree leaned over slightly. Now this was quite a feat because it was made from such stiff wire, and it would have been hard for someone to even physically bend that tree to make it move. When Mom died, it became more noticeable and the whole top of the tree bent right over and the little Lucite star on the top dropped off and lay like a crystal teardrop at the foot of the tree. It was almost as if her tiny tree reacted to her death."

Rhonda D., California, Aerospace Industry

A freeway shooting could mean disaster for an innocent family.

"Our family had the most incredible experience when my husband was working at a military base in Long Beach. I had gone to pick him up at approximately 10 p.m. with our daughter Jennifer, who was about four years old. Jennifer made a very strange request: "Momma, I want to sit behind you tonight." I let her do it, of course, but remember thinking it was odd because she always sat beside me.

On the way, I began to feel my father's presence very strongly in the car, but he had died the previous October. I was thinking, "I wonder what he's doing here with us?" Without any warning, two shots shattered the window on the passenger side and all the glass fell into the front seat. I was in shock: someone had shot at us! The freeway shootings were very common at that time, but you never think it's going to happen to you personally! We now believe without a doubt that our family was taken care of by my dad and the angels he was keeping company with."

Sam S., Arizona, Police dispatcher

Did David help save his sister?

Sam was living in Australia and had an old gas stove in her unit. (Apartments and condominiums are referred to as units in Australia.) To use the oven, she would pull out the door, and a button could be pushed inward on the bottom part of the oven door that would ignite it. She turned the oven on, and the phone rang just then, so she went to answer it before coming back to open the oven door. What Sam didn't know was that the button had been stuck in the "on" position and gas was rapidly building up inside the oven while she was gone to answer the phone. "I went back into the kitchen when I got off the phone, I took a wooden match and leaned inside the oven to light the flame in the back as I always had done. What an explosion! The strange thing is that I know explosions happen instantaneously, and what I saw was like an event in slow motion. I saw a blue ball of flame coming at me, felt myself being pulled back out of the oven, and while of course I couldn't stop the blowup, I was not injured nearly as badly as I might have been.

The eyelashes and eyebrows on the right side of my face, my hair on the right side, and my right arm were burned, but not my eyes! My doctor was astounded and told me "I can't believe you weren't burned more seriously." He said the patterns of the other burns showed that my eyes should have been damaged, and they were just fine! He thought it was miraculous that I had escaped without far more severe injuries.

Well, I knew what it was. After all, I had felt myself being pulled back in a microsecond, faster than what I could have done reacting on my own. I was clearly being helped--it may have been a guardian angel, or it may have been my brother who was looking out for me. This event happened on the anniversary of David's death, a brother who was always very close to me. Whoever pulled me out made all the difference!"

Everyone who looks to a father as the one who can make everything right knows that age doesn't matter. Your dad is the one who will help you out whether you are 5, 25, or 45 years old. The following stories show that dads don't give up that duty when they die, and in fact are still on the job when they aren't physically around.

Mary S., Arizona, Physical Therapist

Mary is convinced that her deceased father gets her safely home.

"I had driven a friend home when the weather was bad, but I didn't realize HOW bad until I got on the freeway outside of town. The roads were basically a sheet of ice, and I had about 15 miles to go. I was really terrified about getting home. Suddenly, I felt like my father was right in the front seat of the car talking to me although he had been dead for four years. His presence was so strong! He was always proud of how he had taught me to drive and constantly gave me driving tips no matter how old I got.

It was like I felt his voice saying things like, "Accelerate into this curve now, but slow down for that one ahead," "Watch out for that truck--he'll suck you in--so back off and move over there." It was absolutely the most incredible thing that I have ever experienced; I felt coached every step of the way, and I know that I was being told things that I wasn't aware of on my own.

When I finally got home, my husband took one look at my face and said, "What happened to you? Are you O.K.?" I smiled tearfully back and told him, "I'm fine...I've just spent the last half hour with my dad." It's hard to put into words the intensity of that feeling of his being there beside me, and I'm convinced that something like this can happen to people."

Carol T., Florida, Administrator

Carol believes her father's assistance brings her safely to her destination.

"I was driving a long trip after dark one time from Pensacola, Florida to Albany, Georgia and found myself becoming very uneasy and finally quite afraid. The back country roads are extremely isolated and after Dothan, Alabama there isn't even anywhere to stop and ask directions. I wasn't sure that I was on the right road and of course, my cell phone was useless where there aren't any cell towers. I was alone, nervous, and afraid of being lost.

I felt like my father (who had died long before this trip) was there protecting me and making sure that I got to my destination. He had been in a nursing home before his death and hadn't driven at all in the last years of his life, although he had liked to drive. The sense that he was there with me was overpowering and made me feel so grateful and much less afraid. I finally arrived exactly where I needed to be, a little late, but safe and sound.

I had a dream right after that and in my dream, dad was driving a car and he took my hand. The sensation was so strong that even as I awoke, I could still feel his touch. I have absolutely no doubt in my mind that he indeed had been driving with me, and although my hands were physically on the wheel, that it was Dad who brought me safely where I needed to be."

Ellan W., Arizona, Administrative Assistant

An agonizing death...but reassurance afterward!

Ellan's beloved husband Jim was diagnosed with pancreatic cancer, and no one could have prepared Ellan or her ten-year-old son for the agonizing progression of this most virulent of cancers...surgery, intensive care stays, staph infection, feeding tubes, seizures, morphine injections, respiratory difficulties, massive drops in blood pressure, and finally hospice. Doctors at that point said he would last from three days to three months; realistically, they didn't expect him to live for more than 48 hours. But Jim was a fighter and told his doctors, "I'll last longer than three months." True to his word, he survived for three months and three days.

Two strange things happened at the time of Jim's death. On the day he died, a few hours before it happened, Ellan was convinced that her husband shook her shoulder as she dozed. When she opened her eyes, no one was there, but she somehow believed her husband's hand had touched her. The day after Jim's death, she felt a pressure on her hand and was again convinced that he had touched her.

The most unusual thing of all happened after Jim died. When the family returned from California where they had gone to scatter Jim's ashes at his request, every picture in the house was off the wall and lying on the floor. A brief investigation showed that no other family member had been in the house, and no one was playing a joke on them. Ellan and Jim had a favorite picture of John Wayne that had been a kind of private joke between the two of them during the more than 12 years of their marriage. John Wayne's picture began moving around the house and would pop up in the strangest places. Other things moved around the house in and out of her bedroom and her son's bedroom on a regular basis.

When Ellan's brakes failed on her white van, she managed to make it safely through an intersection and then home. John Wayne's picture was lying in the middle of her bed. It was almost as if Jim were saying to her, "See? I was right there with you, helping you get home in one piece."

Ellan is convinced that Jim was also the one who protected her son when he fell while repelling. No one else could explain how he was uninjured.

One final amazing thing occurred when Ellan's dad lay dying. She experienced a vision of a blindingly bright light in her doorway and saw an image of her dead husband in the light. It gave her incredible comfort and a sense that Jim was waiting to welcome her dad into heaven.

Jodie P., Arizona, University Administration

Circumstances change overnight for a lonely young woman.

"I moved to Arizona from Wisconsin, and when I had been here a couple of months, I was terribly depressed. I didn't really know anyone, and I didn't have a lot of friends to do things with. My job didn't pay much, so I was always strapped for money.

One night, I was in a particularly low frame of mind and I found myself talking to my father who had been dead for twenty years. I think I was saying something like, "I don't know if there is anything at all you can do to help me, but if you can, now's the time..." The very next day, my life changed dramatically! A fellow employee at a higher level in the organization told me that she had to move out-of-state and that she would be recommending me for her job. She had been living with her sister-in-law, and due to the move would now be opening up a space for the sister-in-law to take in a new roommate. I got the job that I was recommended for, moved in as the sister-in-law's roommate to share expenses, and made a wonderful new friend.

It gave me a completely renewed lease on life to improve my job situation, get a different home life, and start interacting with a new group of people. I can't prove that my dad did this, but I believe that this couldn't have been just luck or some kind of random circumstances coming together. I think someone had my best interests at heart and influenced events in a way that I was helped tremendously, which ultimately gave me hope and strength."

Linda D., New York, Speaker/Trainer

Linda's vision...a comforting sight on the way to a memorial service.

Linda's friend, Jeannette, died at 41 of a metastasized brain tumor and even though gravely ill, Jeannette was the one who became the consoler and comforter to friends and family members at the end. Her death was a shock to all who knew her because of her tremendous strength; people felt if anyone could survive cancer, she could.

Linda was spending a lot of time grieving and crying, and she heard her friend's voice inside her head saying, "If you don't stop crying, I'm going to smack you. What are you doing, being like all of them? (That meant all her Italian relatives.) Do you believe in an afterlife or don't you?" Linda had to finally say, "Please stop! I'm getting a headache."

All of Jeannette's wonderful friends had decided to gather in Central Park for a memorial where they would exchange happy memories of their friend and give symbolic offerings. Linda was riding a bus on the way to the ceremony and was gazing out a window when she saw a wondrous thing just floating out in the sky. There was an image of a thin Jeannette with beautiful hair in a long blue robe. This amazed Linda because at the end, Jeannette had gained weight and lost her hair from the chemotherapy.

She had her arms full of things as if she were carrying them. Linda was tremendously comforted by seeing this ephemeral image but could not explain where it had come from. Slowly, it simply faded from view, but the memory of this happy, smiling vision of her friend sustained Linda during any of the times she felt sad about losing her friend.

Lori G., Arizona, Artist

A brother's visit...but a year after he died?

"I had the most amazing thing happen to me about a year after my brother died. We were very close, and I took his death extremely hard. Especially because the circumstances were quite difficult; he had been murdered during a robbery. On this unusual night, I had checked on my three-month-old daughter in bed and went into the kitchen. There was my brother sitting at the kitchen table just like he used to.

The strange thing is that this seemed completely normal. I wasn't frightened and I wasn't thinking that I was dreaming. It seemed completely acceptable that my deceased brother would be in my kitchen at 3 a.m. He told me that he had come to see Kate (the new baby) and that he was alright. We chatted for a few minutes before my mother-in-law called down from upstairs and asked if I was okay and who was I talking to? This may be the one thing that makes me know that I didn't imagine this whole thing. If someone else heard voices too, then it couldn't be a figment of an overactive imagination. It was very sweet and comforting, and I felt very lucky to have been given this tremendous gift."

Janet B., Arizona, Accounting

Janet's nephew may have saved her life.

Janet was shopping one time on a "day she felt good..." Still grieving over the murder of a beloved nephew on Christmas Eve, she admittedly had "some good days and some bad days."

On this "good day," Janet was leaving the parking lot when an overpowering sense of Rob washed through her. It was so strong that she felt incapable of continuing, so she stopped the car abruptly. Up until that moment, she hadn't been thinking specifically of him that day.

Just then, a truck sped out from behind the two vans parked ahead of her. The laughing kids inside were cutting across the parking lot at an angle and never stopped to check for cross-traffic. Janet stared in horror, realizing that had she not abruptly stopped, she would have been right in the path of the truck. She would have been broadsided at high speed and been badly injured or worse.

Janet describes it as, "Rob simply must have been watching over me that day. The sensation that he was there was what had startled me into stopping the car. If I had had him on my mind that day, it wouldn't have seemed so out-of-the-blue. But because he came to me so powerfully, without warning, tells me there really was an intent to protect me."

Amber W., Arizona, Non-profit Agency

A nephew in trouble is aided by a loving uncle.

"When my brother was eight years old, he tumbled out of a huge tree. It was a miracle he didn't break arms, legs, or his head; as he seemed to miss all the large branches on the way down. He landed in a pile of pine needles, mud, and moss, just barely escaping hitting a big rock. He was unconscious approximately five minutes. As he was coming to, he was positive that he heard a voice saying distinctly, "You're alright. Uncle Russ caught you..." He told us later that he was certain he heard the voice. But our Uncle Russ had been dead for six years!"

Lynne T., Florida, Lobbying Industry

Lynne's cousin John brings comfort in a family crisis...years after his death!

"My son Michael was born premature with many physical problems. Even as an infant he required several surgeries, and each time he seemed so frail and helpless that we just weren't sure that he would make it. When he was slightly more than a year old, I was pregnant again with Thomas, my younger son. That was the year that my cousin John died, a man I felt very close to. I could not attend John's funeral because it was a high-risk pregnancy, and I had been ordered to stay in bed by my doctor. I would never have guessed that I would be given an opportunity to see him several years afterward.

Three years later, Michael came down with severe bacterial meningitis including a fever of 106 degrees. His life was in extreme jeopardy; doctors said that even if he survived, there could be resulting deafness or loss of vision. On a break from watching over him at the hospital, I was at home lying down with baby Thomas at my side. I was crying with deep, wrenching sobs feeling so afraid for that special child I loved so much.

Suddenly, the most intense feeling permeated the room. I was startled but not frightened, and became overwhelmed with a loving presence. A brightness appeared above us, and I distinctly saw my cousin John bathed in the brilliant white light. I thought I might be imagining this until I saw the reaction of the baby beside me. Thomas stared straight upward with huge wide-open eyes and chortled with delight. Clearly, he was seeing the vision although he couldn't know what it meant.

John spoke to me saying, "Please don't cry. Everything will work out alright." His presence was so incredibly affirming to me that I believed what he said and knew that Michael would come out of his crisis safely. Indeed, it happened just that way and today Michael is an active, healthy 11-year-old. He calls his Uncle John (whom he never really knew) his special angel."

God allows people to receive a presence that can be comforting in times of extreme stress. Why this can be the spirit of a family member rather than an angel isn't clear, but the result is always a sense of peace during the resolution of a troublesome situation. What is certain is that the love that is shared during an earthly existence does not extinguish at the time of death. God gives a great gift in allowing this interaction to take place, but it is clearly at His discretion. It isn't something we should expect as a matter of course, but recognize it always is a special favor.

Reflect and Act

Reflect:

- How have you experienced the presence or love of someone who has died, and what does that teach you

about the enduring power of love beyond physical separation?
- Are there any ways that grief shaped your understanding of "connection," and how might you embrace the idea that love continues even when someone is no longer physically present to you?

Act:

- Think of specific things you could do to become more aware of subtle signs, feelings, or energies that may communicate love, guidance, or comfort from those who are no longer physically with you. Is it a smell associated with them? Is it music that has special meaning? Do you feel a hug or touch from someone who is not physically there?
- Think of practices—quiet reflection, prayer, or mindful observation—that can help you tune into the intangible ways that love or spiritual presence reaches you.

9

THE MESSAGES IN DREAMS

Some people believe that dreams should be carefully examined and interpreted using symbols and common understandings. Some believe that dreams are a sort of "brain dump" containing a jumbled re-enactment of stimuli that was registered but not consciously given attention to trying to arrange itself into a logical order. Some believe that dreams should be written down and remembered, even going to the extent of keeping paper and pen handy to make notes as soon as becoming conscious. Others say they have never been able to remember any dream they have ever had. People find their dreams to have every quality from stressful to fun to sexual to frightening to tiring. There are even those who look for omens and portents in their dreams.

While anything described above could be possible, the true importance and relevance of a dream is very personal to the individual who experiences it. In a nonconscious state we may be more open to information that we block when we are in a conscious, waking state. Certain individuals claim to have some kind of "psychic ability" and believe that they are given specific knowledge of future events in dreams.

To the extent that people do receive knowledge of an event that later happens, it must be for their own good or for the good of others involved, which God may allow for His own reasons. In some of the stories related next, the people concerned were not always immediately aware of the significance of their dreams but later learned of their relevance.

The first story tells about how the lives of three people were affected by a dream that warned of an event that could have been fatal to all.

~

Julie R., California, Real Estate/Property Management

Julie's strange dream may have saved three women in a car.

"I had a very dramatic dream about a blue car coming around a blind curve at the bottom of our driveway and causing a terrible accident. It was quite specific and clear. About a week after this dream, I was in the car leaving the house with my mother and my sister, who was driving. I was in the back seat, and as we got to the bottom of the driveway, I momentarily relived that dream and grabbed my sister's shoulder, squeezed it painfully, and screamed, "Don't move! There's a blue car coming around that corner!"

My sister and mother looked at me like I was crazy, but this pause was just long enough to see how a potential accident could happen. In front of our startled and then horrified eyes, a blue car did indeed roar around the corner and race past us, and we realized that if we had pulled out, we would have been broadsided. The resulting accident could definitely have meant serious injury or death for any of the people in our car."

Julie related a second story that is interesting enough for what happened to her, but when linked to an event experienced by her brother and his friends becomes even more intriguing. As Julie tells it, "My father, who was a contractor by profession, built for the family a beautiful house on what had once been Indian land. He was only the second owner, having purchased it from the farmer who had worked the land for many years before that.

Originally, in the early years of California, this land had belonged to the Ohlone-Costanoan Indians, and we know that they had once lived in the area where our home was built because of the number of artifacts that we found during the building process. When the workers dug the hole for the water tank behind the house, they uncovered an unusually large number of utensils, arrowheads, and other telltale remnants of daily Indian life. We had a nearby stream where the large rocks on the shore had hollowed-out places probably caused by the pounding of stones upon clothing or corn as the women cooked and cleaned for the community members.

I don't know if our presence in any way disturbed the Indians who had once lived here, but I did have a bizarre experience two years after we moved in. I was only 19 years old when I awoke one time in the middle of the night in my large bedroom at the back of the house. Standing in my doorway was a tall, male Indian maybe 6"1' with long (about shoulder-length) hair, dressed in a fringed leather jacket and pants. He also had a feather hanging down one side of his hair. He did not move or speak, or even have any facial expression, but simply stood silently.

My heart jumped into my throat and beat so hard it thumped in my chest, but I did not want to move or try to get out of bed to go past him out of the room. Eventually, he faded away and I went back to sleep. This occurred several times the same way, but I never said anything to anyone about it for fear of sounding crazy.

Then something weird happened. I happened to be visiting at home when I overheard my brother and his friends saying something about that "strange Indian at night..." I pressed them further and discovered that my brother who moved into that bedroom when I left home had also seen the Indian visitor, and his friends had seen the Indian as well when they stayed over at night. None of them had ever said anything either, thinking that it sounded too strange to be believable. They were astonished that I had had the same experience they did, only many years earlier. We think that maybe we disturbed a sacred place when we built our home (since Indian grave sites had been found in the nearby Coyote Hills area), and this person is the lone sentinel of a former way of life. He has never threatened or harmed any of us, or in any way interacted with us; he simply maintains some kind of silent vigil that we cannot understand. I don't think he was just a dream of mine because for my brother and his friends to have the same dream would be impossible."

Regina C., Georgia, Police Officer

A family in danger...will the hidden fire be discovered?

Regina's story is an interesting example of how, even if we receive information in dreams, it will be useless if we aren't attentive to other promptings we might receive. As a police officer, Regina is sworn to protect and care for others whenever possible. In this story that happened in her own family, the "protector" could have failed if she hadn't paid attention to the inner urgings she experienced.

"The Labor Day fire in our house shouldn't have been a surprise. After all, I had been dreaming for two weeks before that...the same dream every night. I would wake up drenched in a cold sweat in fear of the fire raging in the house. Each time, I would get up shaking, and search the quiet, peaceful household checking everything, thinking I was missing something. The terror was so real it was crushing. And yet, each time I found nothing and returned to bed, thinking "What's wrong with me that this keeps coming?"

My workload that Labor Day was as usual. What wasn't typical was the bad feeling that clung to me like wet clothing, annoying me constantly. I couldn't call to check on my kids because the phone lines were still down from the horrendous storm the previous night. I told myself that it was perfectly normal for a mother to worry about the children being alone in the house, and the bad feeling came from the fact that I couldn't check on them as I would have liked to.

At one point in the early afternoon, the uneasiness that I couldn't shake suddenly ratcheted up several notches and I decided to leave early and get home to see the kids. As I walked in the door, everything seemed perfectly calm and ordinary, the scattered toys, games, and books were normal, and the television was on. Momentarily lulled, I decided that things were just as they should be and my anxiety was unwarranted.

I had been in the house barely five minutes when I thought I smelled smoke. Sniffing intently, I decided this was NOT my imagination and frantically began checking for a source. It didn't take me long to discover that the heat pump was burning, and when I pulled back the grate, the unit was fully engaged. Leaping into action, I herded the children out and called 911 on my cell phone. Thank God for the cell phone...since the landlines weren't working.

The 911 operator, upon learning who was on the other end of her line, said "I think the volunteer fire department is training in the woods right beside your house there. I'll see if I can get them on the radio." She did, and the volunteer fire team arrived in literally two minutes. The fire was contained in a very short time with the only damage being to the heat pump unit and the area around it inside the wall. There was no damage to any other part of the house or to the children. The insurance company replaced the heat pump, because the source of the fire was faulty wiring which shouldn't have existed in a four-year-old house.

The scariest part for me was when I realized that the back door to the house was blocked from a huge pine tree that had blown over in the previous night's storm, and the burning heat pump was located near the front door. The children would not have had an escape route through either door and didn't have a phone to call for help. They could have perished if the fire had spread quickly and they had panicked.

I am convinced that God gave me warnings, especially the day of the fire, and kept prompting me to get to my home in time. I will be grateful every day for the rest of my life."

Sherry G., Arizona, Office Specialist

Sherry dreams of her father as the family travels back from his funeral.

Sherry's father died quite unexpectedly while he was on a business trip to his native Venezuela, and the family members living in Arizona went down for the funeral. This death was very hard on an extremely close-knit family, and after an extended stay in South America, they were returning home via Miami after 19 days.

Because they had to stay overnight to take an early flight out, the family was at an airport hotel where Sherry was in the same bed as her mother. Because of extreme fatigue, the long flight, and emotional stress, the group had a difficult time falling asleep, and it was well after 2 a.m. before Sherry dozed off.

Quite suddenly, she saw herself at a door and her father was standing there. She was very excited and spoke happily to him about wanting to call the other family members to see and talk to him. He cautioned her not to do that saying, "I'm not really here, so don't call them since I cannot stay and must go now." He was dressed in a dark suit and a hat and simply stood in the doorway. The more Sherry urged him to stay, the more he insisted that it was not possible. Abruptly, Sherry woke up and found herself standing shivering in the doorway of the hotel room with the door wide open.

As she returned to bed, and again laid down to sleep, her mother was mumbling incoherently to her in her father's voice. Sherry spoke to her, but her mother just continued to mutter unintelligibly and then turned over so Sherry could hear nothing further.

She told the family this story, and it seemed as strange as her father's remarks before he left on the business trip. As he had dropped her off at her library job one day, he mysteriously said to her, "I'll be leaving soon, so I want you to take care of your mother, sisters, and brothers." "What do you mean, Poppy?", she asked him, but he never replied.

Sherry has grieved for so long, missing her father, but periodically she hears a cheerful story that helps with her loss. One such story recently came from her sister in Venezuela. Sherry's 20-month-old niece went with her mother (Sherry's sister) to visit her father's grave, and a funny thing happened. While the mother prayed, the toddler laughed and giggled, ran back and forth, made talking sounds, and held out her arms as if she were playing with someone. When they returned home, the little girl grabbed a picture of her grandfather, kissed it, and exclaimed excitedly, "Grandpa, grandpa" leading her mother to believe that perhaps she had seen someone in the cemetery who was not visible to others.

Sarah B., Missouri, Federal Agency

After an abusive relationship, Sarah's dream is about the man she would marry.

Sarah informed me that she told this story to very few people because she thought nobody would believe that this could happen.

"I lived a pretty wild and exciting life for a while, but got to the point where I wanted to settle down and share my life with someone else, so I prayed for someone to come into my life. But I didn't want him to be boring, so I prayed that he would be exciting too, and could even be a little on the wild side.

When that exact person appeared in my life, people should know that they had better be careful about what they pray for, because I got someone a little too dangerous. I had 18 months of "hell" from a person who became abusive and alcoholic.

This was not what I had prayed for! I even lost my home because it was the only way I could escape, to just walk away and go live with my family. I did ultimately sue him and received a good sum of money, but what was most important was that I learned my lesson.

I changed my prayer to asking for a good person who could enrich my life and allow me to enrich his, someone I could love in a truly special way. What happened next is amazing.

A woman I had not seen in several years called unexpectedly to simply reconnect. She invited me to come for a visit, so I took a bus to her town. I fell asleep on that bus and had the most incredible dream. I saw a bowling alley and a man walked in that I knew would be my future husband. I saw his clothes, heard his voice, knew how he looked, and knew his name! I heard our conversation word for word.

When my friend suggested during my visit that I accompany her on her weekly bowling night, the entire dream came flooding back, unfolding like a movie inside my head. When a member of my friend's bowling team walked in to join us, there he was! Without being introduced, I said, "Hello Carey." This was the man of my dreams and was the one who is now my husband. All the former restlessness and desire for excitement is no longer important; what really matters is a family, a home, and a very unique kind of love. Life is good!

I think God played a part in bringing us together and that makes our relationship even more extraordinary and very, very special."

Kristy H., Minnesota, Non-Profit Service Agency

Kristy's dream prevents her from attending a dangerous party.

"I had a guy at my school that I had gotten to know for about a year. We had started talking to each other in the library at school, then spent a lot of time on the phone, and had done a few things like go to the movies but had a strictly platonic relationship. He was funny and amusing to hang out with.

One night I had a strange dream about my friend. In this dream we were watching movies in a movie theater but the seats were all mattresses and about twenty people were paired off lying on different mattresses. I was paired off with Bob, the friend I mentioned above. In my dream, Bob began to sexually assault me, and I was trying to fight him off.

I awoke when the phone rang, and it was Bob who had called me to invite me to a Halloween party. I told him I thought that would be fun until he told me more about it. Bob said that he wanted to do a movie marathon in his room, and we would all keep watching until everybody was tired, and then if we wanted, we could just lie down and have a sleepover.

Now this was a huge red flag for me since the memory of that scary dream was still so vivid! I told Bob that I would think about the party, but in my heart, I knew that I would not go.

I finally cut off the relationship not long after that when he revealed some things about himself that made me very uncomfortable. Bob told me over the phone one day that he had molested his own sister and been thrown out of the house by his parents. He finally died at the age of nineteen or twenty. I know it sounds strange, but I was somewhat relieved that he wouldn't be able to hurt anyone else."

Leona C., Arizona, Production Specialist-Technical Environment

Leona receives a unique opportunity to say goodbye.

"The strangest dream I ever had, over twenty years ago, ended up creating an amazing string of consequences in my life. In my dream, I walked into an all-white room (sheets, bed, everything was white) and saw a tiny, frail person with white hair, but couldn't tell if it was a man or a woman. I sat down in the chair by the bed and put my hand down on the sheets. A small hand crept out from under the blanket and covered mine, and with it came a tremendous sense of peace and tranquility.

The next day, I received a phone call about a friend who had passed away, and I was convinced that my dream had been about this friend.

However, several weeks later, my aunt came to visit and said my grandmother (her mother) was very sick and she planned to go to Philadelphia to be with her. A little voice inside my head told me, "You go too," so right then I decided to go with my aunt.

When we walked into my grandmother's hospital room, I was dumbfounded to see the room from my dream, and the frail person in the bed now had a face--it was my grandmother. This was quite a shock to me to see the tiny figure in the bed, because my grandmother had always been a very large and robust woman. She seemed to have aged decades!

As I approached the bed, grandmother opened her eyes and looked at me and said, "I was just talking to your mother (who had been dead for over ten years at this point) and she told me one of the girls would be coming, but I didn't think it would be you." Now, there had been bad feelings between us for a long time, so she was probably referring to the estrangement.

As I bent over to kiss her forehead, I looked deep into her eyes, and it was like being drawn into a very long tunnel...I could see my mother, and all the relatives who had lived before me lined up. The message I heard was so clear, almost as if it had been spoken aloud, "We are all together...we are all one...we are an extension of one another." It felt timeless. The feeling of tremendous peace that I experienced at this point is almost indescribable.

The oddest part of this is that I feel like I was able to say goodbye to my mother in my grandmother's eyes, and this was something I had never been able to say to her physically. She had been killed by a drunk driver, and I never had a chance to see her before she died. This was especially hard for me because there had also been some bad feelings and words between us, and this had left a lot of unfinished baggage for me. Any of the hard feelings between my grandmother and me were also erased at this moment. All was finally healed."

Julie S., Arizona, Department of Public Safety

A young wife's "vision" in the night turns out to have been a real person.

"We had a very dear family friend who had died from a motorcycle accident in Saudi Arabia. Approximately ten years later, our son brought his new wife to our house for the weekend. They had been married for less than a year at that point. A very strange thing happened their first night visiting as they were sleeping in the master bedroom. Our daughter-in-law began screaming hysterically in the middle of the night because she had been awakened to see someone at the foot of their bed. This was very real to her and she gave a vivid, detailed description of the person who stood watching them as they slept.

After she calmed down, she admitted that she had been badly frightened only because it was so startling to see someone appear whom she thought had broken into the house. Later, as she realized that this was not a burglar, she said that the apparition didn't seem to want to harm them, but rather appeared to have a more protective, interested, and friendly demeanor.

As my daughter-in-law talked about the person she had seen, my son and I just stared at each other in shock...it was a perfect description of our close friend. In fact, I went through some boxes of old pictures and found one to show her and she said that, indeed, that was the very person she had seen. We felt this was pretty remarkable and don't have any way to explain how or why something like this would happen."

Judith H., Wisconsin, Church Secretary

Judith's dream convinces her to look for other houses.

"I feel very strongly that the Lord spoke to me in a dream one time. My husband and I were house hunting, and we had finally decided on a particular house. We made a down payment with final purchase contingent upon the approval of our VA loan.

Right after that, I had a very compelling dream. I seemed to be seeing all kinds of other houses and possibilities that we hadn't looked at. My feeling was that we shouldn't limit ourselves to the house we had the down payment on. I told my husband about my dream and my feelings the very next day. He responded pragmatically, "Well, if we aren't supposed to have this house, our loan won't be approved. Then we'll get our down payment back."

That is exactly what happened! When the loan was not approved, we took our down payment and looked at other houses. We then found the house we are living in now and the loan was approved with no difficulty for a house we love. I am convinced that we were steered away from the other one."

Amy K., Birmingham England, Receptionist

A dream foretells the loss of a love for Amy.

"When I was 18 years old, I fell deeply in love with someone that my family did not approve of. Apparently, his family had some of the same feelings. I had a very strange dream three nights in a row that was identical each night.

I dreamed I was losing him, and he was fading away from me. In the dream he said, "Don't be angry, you can't do anything about this." I felt hands holding me back as I struggled and it was pitch black around me in this dream. A week after the third dream, his parents abruptly left their home and took him away somewhere and we have never had any further contact since. To this day, I do not know where in the world he or his family is." As Amy told this story, her eyes brimmed with tears, and I could see that the pain is as real today--eight years later--as it was when she lost this "true love." She has never cared for anyone else as deeply since, and is still going through a grieving process. This is an open-ended story because no one knows where Amy will be led in the future to complete this unfinished relationship and continue with her life. She may be reunited with this person in the future, or she may never encounter him again.

Cynthia C., Illinois, Port Authority District

A mother's dream of trouble for her daughter is quite accurate, but not exactly as she imagined it.

"I had a very odd dream in which I saw a meteorologist doing a weather report that focused on Charleston, South Carolina and reported very severe weather, with a potential hurricane coming. I have a 22-year-old daughter stationed with the Navy there, so I felt I needed to call her.

When I checked the weather, I discovered that there was nothing wrong with Charleston, but there was still a tremendous sense of urgency from the dream. It was so vivid that I went ahead and called my daughter to ask if she was alright.

My daughter told me that there was no hurricane or bad weather there, but indeed things were not as they should be. She was in trouble on the base for some infraction of rules, and she would never have called to tell me about that. She wouldn't have volunteered information like that, but because I asked, she did talk to me about it. I really appreciated the dream that clued me in that something was wrong for my child."

Eleni M., Oregon, Police Department

An odd match in timing surprises Eleni.

"A very odd coincidence occurred regarding a school friend of mine. I had only been out of high school for a couple of years and I was working at a Fred Meyer store at the time. I had a strange dream that the mother of a school friend who was one grade lower had died. Now I had only met this woman on two occasions. In my dream, I looked at a clock and saw that it was 1 a.m.

I happened to see that friend sometime later and was told that her mother's father had died on the day and at the time that I had dreamed about them. I thought this was a most unusual circumstance."

Rita D., Colorado, Education

Rita is told to pray for her father.

"When I was just 11 years old, I had a dream in which I was in a cabin with my relatives, and we were all taking a nap in bunk beds. My mother was on one side of me, I was in the middle, and my sister and her child were on the other side. Jesus appeared to me and told me to pray for my family, but I have always done this anyway.

In another more recent dream, I saw an angel, a hazy light-filled male figure who said to me, "Pray for your father while he is still alive. You will no longer see him after the spring," and in fact, he did die the following spring. I think that I have accepted his passing better because I received a kind of advance notice. I do not believe I would have taken it as well if there had been no warning."

Kay O., Minnesota, Non-Profit Agency

Kay has learned to look to her dreams for important information.

Kay has experienced many interesting dreams over the years, but three of them stand out in her mind as being influenced by something far beyond her own consciousness. She believes that she was alerted to potential dangers through these dreams, all of which later came true.

"I saw my daughter lying on a surgery table one time, and about a month after that dream, she really did have emergency surgery. What they thought was an abscessed tooth was a tumor that had to be removed.

So, it didn't surprise me when I dreamed that my husband's grandmother had a woman dressed in black standing at the foot of her bed, and then the grandmother died the following morning. I began to put a great deal of trust in anything that I dreamed about.

In one dream, I saw my husband die while jumping from rock to rock in a small stream during one of our camping trips. When he really did start doing that while we were out in the woods, I got really mad at him and made him stop immediately. Over the years, I have learned to pay attention to those unusual messages in the night."

Mary Elizabeth A., Oregon, Kindergarten Teacher

A healing dream of love helps a woman regain balance.

"I have been interested in angels for a long time. While I was in the South of France alone for three weeks, thinking that my marriage was falling apart, I had some amazing dreams. The first one was terrifying, and as I awoke from it, I prayed the 23rd Psalm over and over. Then I fell back to sleep and began to see childhood memories as if I was watching a movie, first as a baby and then as a toddler. I saw a wonderful loving presence and went over to this figure and crawled up on its lap. I felt engulfed by love and a beautiful golden light and felt like I was going through a tunnel of light. I believed that the message of the dream was about learning to love again.

In the morning, I opened the shutters to a beautiful dawn, the most magnificent sunrise I had ever seen and I felt healed. I wrote letters to some of my family members that day, and was guided to a new church in Seaside where the minister and his wife were exactly the friends I needed at that point in my life.

When I returned, even my husband realized I was different, since this was a really life-changing event for me."

Reflect and Act

Reflect:

- Have you ever had a dream that, in hindsight, seemed to hold guidance, warning, or insight? How did it affect your understanding of the unseen ways God communicates?

- How do you usually respond to your dreams—dismiss, analyze, or ponder—and what might that reveal about your openness to subtle spiritual messages?

Act:

- Learn specific practices that could help you become more attentive to dreams, such as keeping a dream journal or setting an intention before sleep to receive guidance.
- How can you discern whether a dream carries meaningful insight or guidance, versus random mental activity, without losing trust in your intuition or spiritual perception?

10

GOD'S SPECIAL GIFT: GRANDPARENTS

The following stories are heartwarming examples of the love of grandparents for their grandchildren. Both grandmothers and grandfathers have played a key role for other family members during their lives and even after their deaths, proving again that love can surpass any barrier, even time. An interesting pattern is how the grandparent will appear at a time of crisis for the family member usually bringing some kind of comfort or consolation that cannot be achieved otherwise.

Ruth M., Florida

Ruth's grandmother brings her comfort.

"When I was growing up, I believed that my mother's parents loved me more than anyone else. Their love seemed so absolute and unconditional. My beloved grandmother died in 1983 and I know she visited me when I had my son Joey in 1985. I was living at my parents' house at the time, quite ill both physically and emotionally, because my husband had decided he didn't want a wife and baby. I remember lying on the bed shortly after Joey was born feeling quite miserable and wondering what I should do with my life. My beautiful newborn son rested quietly in the bassinet beside me.

Suddenly I felt a presence. I immediately recognized the scent of the powder my grandmother had worn, so I knew it was she. I heard her voice murmuring, "Joey is a beautiful baby. Everything will be all right; you'll see. I love you." I felt the hair brushed off my forehead, and the lightest touch of a kiss on my cheek. As suddenly as she had come, she was gone.

What remained was a deep sense of well-being and peace flooding through me. Of course she was right, everything would work out somehow, some way... In that instant, after having been so depressed I was ready to doubt the existence of God, I KNEW that God was real, God was love, and God was a part of my life.

What was fascinating was the reaction of the few people I talked to about this. All of my family members seemed to react differently.

My mother said: "She was MY mother, why on earth would she come to you?" My Uncle Jimmy (my mother's brother) told me: "I believe your story; that sounds exactly like her. And she loved you very much, Ruth." My Aunt Alice (grandma's sister) added: "My mother visited my daughter at a time when she needed her. I guess the women of our family cross when they're needed." Sister Mary Ruth–a Sister of Saint Joseph (my mother's sister) said: "She loved you Ruth, why wouldn't she come when you needed her? I don't believe heaven and earth are as separate as people think. Love doesn't stop at death."

Ruth's grandfather also gave her an unusual sign after his death. Six months afterwards, the pink flowers were an unmistakable message for Ruth.

"My grandfather's death was a blessing really, since he had been ill for some time before that. We had an interesting conversation shortly before he died. He told me, "I may not make it to heaven; I've done some bad things in my life. I hope you'll love me anyway." I responded, "Don't be silly. Our God is a God of love and you are a good man. I'm sure heaven is waiting for you. And of course I'll always love you. When I was growing up, I felt that you and Grandma were the only ones who truly loved me. Your love got me this far, so of course you'll always have it." There is a very lengthy continuation of this story that leads up to the appearance of the pink flowers at the end. (the flowers are the unusual sign…)

Grandpa still seemed troubled, "I assume I'm going to die soon, that's what this is leading up to. Will you be alright?" I tried to reassure him, "Grandpa, even when you aren't on earth anymore, I'll have your love. I know that you're going to heaven, but you seem to have doubts. So, promise me this: that you will let me know you are alright once you're in heaven."

Grandpa smiled wearily, "I don't know if I'll have the transportation." I said, "Well, grandma visited me after Joey was born, remember? She had been in heaven for two and a half years. Ask her how, if you don't know."

Grandpa seemed calmer after that and promised me that he would let me know that things were okay. I was so glad that I had talked to him to let him know how much he meant to me because the next time I visited, just a few weeks later, he didn't know who I was. A few months after that, he was gone.

I felt a sense of peace when grandpa died. I was positive that he was in heaven. I grieved for MY loss, but not for him, since I knew he was in a better place.

The April after his death, about six months later, I awoke one morning with grandpa strongly on my mind. "Please send me a sign and let me know that you are in heaven," I prayed. That afternoon, when I came home, I saw small pink flowers blooming in my garden. To anyone else this may have seemed inconsequential, but to me...oh, it was so much more than that! Tears filled my eyes, and I was overcome with a sense of peace and love and truly felt grandpa's presence. I had my sign and knew indeed that he was in heaven. Why?

I had planted wildflower seeds on that spot when grandpa died. They had never bloomed. Grandpa had those same flowers in his yard, and they did just fine; several times he had helped me dig up some for transplanting into my yard. I would follow his instructions to the letter; yet the flowers would never take hold and always died a few days later. "Don't worry," he'd tell me, "They'll come back next year." They never did.

Suddenly, there were those precious pink flowers actually blooming in my garden! Tiny, pink flowers...a gift...a sign from grandpa and from God. All you have to do is ask and you shall receive. Well, I had asked, and I had been given my sign.

The next day, the flowers were gone. They never came back. But they didn't need to...I had received the message I wanted."

Julie D., Arizona, Information Systems

A loving grandmother sees her grandchildren after her death.

"My friend had a very unusual thing happen to her one time when she had a new baby in the house in addition to her toddler. Her grandmother, who lived on the other side of the country, had never seen either of her children.

One night she awakened abruptly from a sound sleep to feel a presence, quite loving and comforting, in her room. She even saw an ethereal, shadowy essence that seemed to hover over the infant's crib which was there in her bedroom. The specter began to move in a gliding fashion, out into the hallway. She wasn't afraid at all, but wanted to find out where it was going, so she got up and crept out behind the figure. She followed the shape into her toddler's room and watched silently as it hovered over the sleeping child.

My friend did not feel any fear, only a very kind and benevolent sense. She did not, at that moment, associate it with her grandmother. However, the next morning, she was notified that her grandmother had died the previous night right around the time that the shadowy presence was in her house. My friend was convinced that her grandmother's spirit had come to see the babies before departing. She felt that God had blessed them with a very special gift and something that would have meant a great deal to her grandmother. My friend also said that it meant a lot to her to know that the grandmother had finally seen her beloved grandchildren."

Donna Z., California, Chiropractic Assistant

Donna receives desperately needed encouragement from a strange source.

"I had a miscarriage with my first baby, and it was an unusually violent reaction: terrible bleeding and cramps that required emergency treatment. It was amazing that I had become pregnant in the first place because I had been told that I would never have children.

Something very strange happened to me in the middle of this tremendously emotional situation. I was under anesthesia during the surgery, and I clearly saw my grandmother who died three years ago. She came to my side and generated such a wonderful, loving, and safe feeling that I felt everything would be alright. And that is exactly how things turned out."

Cecelia L., Arizona, Accountant

A young girl's deceased grandfather visits her after his death.

Cecelia's seven-year-old daughter Nicole was extremely close to her grandfather who was dying of cancer. He in fact did die one day at 3:30 p.m., but the babysitter had been instructed not to say anything to the young girl.

Finally, Cecelia decided the next day to break the news gently to the impressionable youngster. Nicole asked, "When did grandpa go away?" Cecelia replied, "Yesterday afternoon." "But Mama," Nicole said with a puzzled voice, "I played with him last night." As the story came out, Cecelia heard something that she could not explain logically. "I had found Nicole sitting and watching a video in the middle of the night, and wondered why Cinderella was so important that she had it on when she should be sleeping.

She told me that next afternoon that her grandpa came in the middle of the night and said "Don't be sad. What would make you happy?" and Nicole said that she wanted grandpa to watch Cinderella with her. And he did, as she told it. I don't know how Nicole could have seen her grandpa when he had died many hours earlier, but I believe my daughter is telling the truth."

Susan W., Arizona, Police Communications

A grandfather's comfort helps Susan's sister.

"My sister found a very unusual thing happening to her after our grandfather died of cancer. She is extremely sensitive, but found that after his death, she felt not sad and mournful, but relieved. Then she began to feel guilty about the fact that she didn't feel sad.

During the night one time, grandfather appeared to my sister and told her that she had nothing to be sorry about, that he knew she loved him, and that everything would be alright. He then kissed her, which she described more as a feeling that a physical touch. One thing that pleased her tremendously was that he had become very frail before he died, and when he appeared to her, grandfather looked quite robust and healthy."

Janet N., Iowa, Optometry

A young man's dying words give his family great comfort.

"My grandfather played an important role in our family when we had a recent death. My nephew, Mitchell, who was just 24 years old, died of cystic fibrosis, which was a very hard thing for our family to go through. As we were gathered around his deathbed, he seemed right at the end to take on a radiant glow in his face as he called out his grandfather's name and held out his arms as if reaching for him.

My dad (Mitchell's grandfather) had been dead for nine years at the time and he and Mitchell had always had an extremely close relationship. We just knew that Mitchell and his favorite grandfather were now happily together in heaven. This knowledge gave the entire family a tremendous sense of joy, peace, and comfort during the days of the funeral, knowing that our loved ones were together. We have grieved in a very different way than we would if that had not happened."

Todd W., Arizona, Forensic Chemist

A grandmother suffering from memory loss recovers the day her great-granddaughter is born and delights in the child for two joy-filled weeks before she dies.

Todd's grandmother suffered from severe short-term memory loss for years, and at one point had a steady and rapid progression of the disease. She couldn't remember from day-to-day that Todd was married or that he was expecting a baby. During one visit, she didn't recognize Todd's wife Wendy, and asked "Who is that woman with you?" Saddened, Todd and Wendy prayed that she would be able to live long enough to see her great-granddaughter born, and to understand that she had one.

"The day Kayla was born, my grandmother suddenly became lucid for the first time in eight years, and she was perfect for the next two weeks. She asked about the baby every single day and absolutely delighted in her great-granddaughter. Everyone in our family thought it was a miracle, and that she was getting better, but just two weeks later she had a stroke and died. We know that her happiness truly brightened those final days, and that it was a tiny miracle that parted the curtain of darkness that had clouded her mind for so long. Those last two weeks were very joyful and loving and gave happy memories to the entire family."

Douglas B., Iowa, Hospitality Industry

Did Douglas know ahead of time about his grandmother's heart problem?

"I think sometimes things happen that don't make sense until afterward when we have more information. For example, one time I woke up with a sudden attack of very severe chest pain that really puzzled me. I'm extremely healthy and have no medical or heart problems at all.

Just a week later, my grandmother died very unexpectedly

from a heart attack. In retrospect, I believe that maybe what I felt was an indication of future events."

Kathryn H., California, Education

A grandmother is helped when she feels very much alone.

My grandmother Fay, who was about 69 years old at the time, was stranded in San Rafael when her car broke down. She climbed over a fence to find help, but whoever she encountered said she would have to leave her car there because they couldn't help her. Then she called a daughter 90 miles away who couldn't do anything either.

So, she started walking, alone, in a strange area. Grandmother finally ended up at a Denny's restaurant and went into the restroom to have a good cry. Thinking, "Oh God, I don't know what to do!" she was sobbing when a woman came in and Fay said, "Don't worry about me" and didn't want to tell her the problem. But the woman, speaking very gently and projecting a strong, calm demeanor repeated, "I really do think you need to tell me what's going on." So, grandmother described her situation, feeling the calm her visitor exhibited coming over her as well. Suddenly everything seemed like it would work out alright, and the situation wasn't so bad after all.

The stranger told Fay that she would drive her home, and Fay felt very at ease and comfortable with her as she was taken all the way back to Ukiah. The woman gave grandmother a name and said she lived in Santa Rosa, but when Fay tried to find an address to send her a small card and gift, there wasn't any such person in Santa Rosa. Grandmother became convinced that a special angel had come to help her in a moment when it looked like she had been deserted."

Laura B., Iowa, Medical Services and Sales

A grandmother is the only one who correctly guesses her grandson's problem.

"Two years ago, my grandson had been having some strange medical problems. He passed out one time when he was riding his bike, and again when he was running a relay race at school. I saw the family for Labor Day, and said to my son and his wife, "Have you had his heart checked out? I think something is wrong with his heart."

The parents assured me that indeed they had the doctors checking out everything possible. In fact, three doctors were looking into it. At that point, they all believed that he was simply hyper-ventilating. But I didn't believe it. I still thought it was his heart.

The day after Labor Day proved me right, but it was a sad way to find that out. My grandson was in a race at school and collapsed, got up and said, "I'm O.K." and then fell again and died on the spot of a heart attack. Looking back, I don't know that there was anything we could have done differently, but I think it was odd that I had such a strong feeling about the problem being with his heart."

Laura feels that people may have warnings or feelings about impending death because of what happened with her father.

"When my dad passed away, I saw him just hours before he died. He seemed fine to me; except he had this terrible urge to get the storm windows up. He almost didn't take time to stop and talk with me because he felt pushed to get the windows in.

It seemed odd to me that there was such an urgency about a task that he could do anytime, but later I decided that maybe he knew he wouldn't be there and didn't want that job left for my mom. In each case, I know that it was the strength of God that allowed me to get through the situations."

Paul S., Alabama, Teacher

Paul's grandfather communicates with him in a most unusual way.

"When I was a junior in high school, I attended a week-long civics clinic camp and was very excited to have some time away from home. The first three days were great, but on Thursday, I awoke a little after four in the morning with a crushing pain in my chest. Nothing seemed to make it go away, not walking around or taking a shower or anything. The group was going on a day-long field trip that day, and I did participate even though I continued to feel sick. As I got off the bus in the afternoon, a counselor pulled me aside and asked me to go to the office.

My mother was waiting there with sad news for me. My grandfather had died early in the morning. When she told me that it had been a heart attack around 4 a.m., the pain in my chest that had troubled me the entire day mysteriously disappeared. In an instant! I couldn't help wondering if my grandfather had been communicating with me.

We were extremely close, and I had spent the weekend preceding my trip with my grandad. When I left on Sunday afternoon, I told him I would see him when I got back. My grandfather said something, that in retrospect, took on new meaning. He had told me "Well, if I don't see you, I'll talk with you." In my excitement about leaving for camp, I just didn't think much of it at the time. Now I became convinced that he had used the pain as a message; I guess it was his way of saying goodbye to me."

Elisa R., Arizona

A loving grandmother visits the new baby.

"My mother died about 10 years before my daughter had a very unusual experience. My daughter had gotten up in the middle of the night to get a drink and sat for a moment on the edge of the bed. She heard footsteps and saw her grandmother coming upstairs. "Nana!" she squealed with delight. "How are you?" asked her grandmother. My daughter murmured, "I'm ok Nana, but my back hurts a little." My mother started rubbing her back and lovingly admired the new baby, her great-granddaughter, who was sleeping nearby. She said in Spanish, "The baby is so beautiful and such a joy." When my daughter told me this later, I became very sentimental and emotional because this daughter of mine was my mother's favorite. Although my daughter thought she might have been dreaming, she told me that her husband woke up while she was speaking with her grandmother and asked her "Who are you talking to?" So then, we realized it couldn't have been a dream.

My father also had a strange encounter. After my mother died, he was sitting in a rocker watching TV which he had always watched with her, and he fell asleep. He dreamed that Mom poked him in the stomach and said, "Why don't you just go to bed?" He woke up abruptly and saw Mom walking into the bedroom, but she was all white. She must have come back in spirit to sit with him by the TV just one more time.

The encounters with grandparents who have passed on are so comforting to people because the connection while they are living is such a special one. The stories in this section demonstrate a powerful love bond like no other and suggest that even death cannot separate grandparents from their families.

Reflect and Act

Reflect:

- How have you seen God's love reflected through the grandparents or elders in your life, especially in ways that provided comfort or guidance beyond what anyone else could offer?
- Can you recall a time of crisis when a grandparent, or someone acting as a God-inspired presence, brought consolation or direction that felt almost like divine intervention or angelic guidance? What does that reveal about God's work through people?

Act:

- How might you intentionally act as an instrument of God's love to support, guide, or comfort <u>younger family members</u> during times of need?
- Decide on ways that you can use your actions and words to leave a lasting impact on your family or community—so that your influence continues as a source of blessing even after you are no longer present.

AFTERWORD

The inspiring stories in this volume remind us of how important it is to look for miracles every day–to stay hopeful, to become more optimistic, to be reminded of our Creator's love for us. We must remember to watch for ways that we can be used in service to others by being in the right place at the right time when we follow a thought or guiding that even we don't fully understand the meaning of. We then become instruments of the Divine partnership that becomes a wonderful "coincidence."

When we experience the blessings described by the people in this book, the only response can be one of gratitude. Take time each day to be thankful for the gifts you receive and they will continue to flow to you with even greater abundance.

INDEX

NAME - STATE - PAGE NUMBER

Adrienne S., Arizona - 33

Alma F., California - 78

Amber W., Arizona - 215

Amy K., Birmingham, U.K. - 233

Amy K., Paraguay - 46

Ann F., Arizona - 154

Anne K., Massachusetts - 82

Annie L., California - 128

Art S., Arizona - 170

Barb B., Arizona - 95

Barbara W., Louisiana - 15

Beatrice L., California - 193

Betty Jo V., Michigan - 142

Bill M., Arizona - 114

"Bill" T., Michigan - 28

Bob R., Arizona - 68

Carol T., Florida - 209

Cathy T., Oregon - 97

Cathy K., California - 119

Cecelia L., Arizona - 244

Cheri C., Washington - 93

Chery A., Texas - 148

Christina O., Arizona - 51

Christina O., Arizona - 136

Chuck B., Arizona - 112

Chuck F., Arizona - 172

Cynthia C., Illinois - 234

Dale C., Arizona - 17

Dawn C., California - 143

Dawn A., Arizona - 85

Deanna S., Florida - 91

Debbie L., Michigan - 116

Deborah B., Birmingham, U.K. - 113

Deborah W., Texas - 188

Deborah F., California - 58

Dennie B., Oklahoma - 93

Diana B., Illinois - 190

Diane J., New Jersey - 13

Dixie A., Wyoming - 125

Donna Z., California - 244

Donna P., Arizona - 185

Dottie R., North Carolina - 81

Douglas B., Iowa - 247

Dr., Bobbe S., California - 20

Elena J., Arizona - 165

Eleni M., Oregon - 235

Elisa R., Arizona - 251

Ellan W., Arizona - 210

Ellie L., Arizona - 132

Erin A., Oregon - 30

Evelyn N., California - 34

Georgia P., Michigan - 140

Ginger V., Arizona - 25

Gwendolyn M., California - 180

Harriet A., Michigan - 126

Iris S., Minnesota - 51

James B., Arizona - 179

Jane B., Massachusetts - 156

Jane M., Arizona - 63

Janet B., Arizona - 214

Janet N., Iowa - 246

Janette S., Adelaide, Australia - 111

Jeana L., California - 90

Jene B., Arizona - 31

Jennifer F., Oregon - 28

JeriAnn, Illinois - 191

Jesse M., Arizona - 168

Jill F., Iowa - 134

Jodie P., Arizona - 211

John R., Arizona - 42

John R., Arizona - 122

Joyce B., Arizona - 56

Joyce W., Minnesota - 48

Judith H., Wisconsin - 232

Julie H., Michigan - 164

Julie D., Arizona - 243

Julie S., Arizona - 231

Julie R., California - 220

June V., Minnesota - 186

Kamila L., Michigan - 8

Karen J., California - 37

Karen B., Birmingham, U.K. - 77

Karen D., Arizona - 115

Karen B., Arizona - 53

Karen S., Michigan - 35

Kathryn H., California - 248

Kathy S., New Mexico - 81

Kathy D., Arizona - 44

Kathy D., Arizona - 183

Kay O., Minnesota - 236

Kelley B., California - 62

Kelley B., California - 103

Keri Lee P., California - 75

Kim N., California - 135

Kim F., Arizona - 166

Kim B., California - 153

Kristi K., Michigan - 83

Kristy H., Minnesota - 228

Larry J., Arizona - 142

Laura Z., Arizona - 6

Laura C., Michigan - 172

Laura B., Iowa - 249

Leona C., Arizona - 229

Linda C., Arizona - 10

Linda C., Wyoming - 204

Linda D., New York - 109

Linda S., Arizona - 177

Linda F., California - 123

Linda D., New York - 212

Lori G., Arizona - 101

Lori G., Arizona - 213

Lorie B., Arizona - 92

Lynn S., Alabama - 151

Lynn L., Minnesota - 129

Lynne T., Florida - 216

Marcia R., Arizona - 59

Margaret K., Louisiana - 198

Maria K., Arizona - 155

Marilyn M., California - 22

Marilyn S., Oregon - 26

Marilyn T., Minnesota - 94

Marilyn G., Minnesota - 19

Mary M., Arizona - 99

Mary T., Wisconsin - 184

Mary S., Arizona - 208

Mary Elizabeth A., Oregon - 237

Mimi B., California - 36

Nancy V., Minnesota - 33

Nancy C., Minnesota - 135

Naomi J., New Mexico - 102

Pam A., Missouri - 138

Pam C., Louisiana - 69

Pam S., Ohio - 89

Pam S., Arizona - 163

Patricia A., New York - 131

Patty Y., Minnesota - 182

Paul S., Alabama - 250

Paula T., Arizona - 26

Pauline Sc., Arizona - 160

Pauline Sa., Arizona - 175

Penny B., Wisconsin - 121

Regina C., Georgia - 223

Renee J., Arizona - 96

Rhonda D., California - 205

Richard D., Arizona - 194

Rick B., Arizona - 181

Rita D., Colorado - 235

Rob M., New Jersey - 152

Robert K., California - 174

Roberta B., Arizona - 24

Robin S., Wisconsin - 108

Roger B., Florida - 176

Ruth M., Florida - 239

Sam S., Arizona - 206

Sara H., Pennsylvania - 129

Sarah B., Missouri - 227

Sherry L., Arizona - 4

Sherry G., Arizona - 225

Susan W., Arizona - 245

Susie V., Oklahoma - 79

Suzi L., California - 84

Terri B., Virginia - 80

Theresa B., Arizona - 49

Tim K., California - 127

Todd W., Arizona - 246

Trena U., Oregon - 174

Victoria F., Arizona - 189

Wendy S., Minnesota - 27

Yolanda C., Arizona - 130

ABOUT THE AUTHOR
PATRICIA CRAMER

Patricia Cramer has spent her career as an international speaker and coach for Management, Supervisory, and Professional groups. She trained and consulted for business and government clients in the United States, Canada, Australia, England, Ireland, and Scotland. Patricia's passion has always been to help people perform at their peak and build skills for their career and professional growth as she taught Management and Leadership Skills, Communication and Listening Skills, Conflict Management, Team Development, Business Writing, Grammar Skills, Managing Multiple Priorities, and Dynamic Presentations. Her educational background supported this work with an M.B.A. in Management, and an M.A. in Counseling/Personnel.

Patricia authored video and audio training programs: Grammar for Business Professionals, Writing Winning Proposals, and Effective Presentation Skills. Her books include: High-Impact Letters, Memos, and E-mails; High-Impact Reports and

Proposals; Business Guide to Proofreading and Grammar; In the Hands of Angels; and 911 to Heaven. Patricia's joy today comes from sharing her books of "miraculous moments" and being editor of an arts and literary magazine published for her local community in southern Arizona.

www.ingramcontent.com/pod-product-compliance
Lightning Source LLC
Chambersburg PA
CBHW071305110426
42743CB00042B/1179